Not~So~ Humble Pies

KELLY JAGGERS

Published by
Adams Media, a division of F+W Media, Inc.
57 Littlefield Street, Avon, MA 02322. U.S.A.
www.adamsmedia.com

Contains material adapted and abridged from *The Everything® Pie Cookbook* by Kelly
Jaggers, copyright © 2011 by F+W Media, Inc., ISBN 10: 1-4405-2726-1, ISBN 13:
978-1-4405-2726-5.

ISBN 10: 1-4405-3291-5
ISBN 13: 978-1-4405-3291-7
eISBN 10: 1-4405-3495-0
eISBN 13: 978-1-4405-3495-9

Printed in China.

10   9   8   7   6   5   4   3   2   1

Library of Congress Cataloging-in-Publication Data
is available from the publisher.

This publication is designed to provide accurate and authoritative information with regard to
the subject matter covered. It is sold with the understanding that the publisher is not engaged
in rendering legal, accounting, or other professional advice. If legal advice or other expert
assistance is required, the services of a competent professional person should be sought.
　　　—From a *Declaration of Principles* jointly adopted by a Committee of the American Bar
　　　　　　　Association and a Committee of Publishers and Associations

Many of the designations used by manufacturers and sellers to distinguish their product are
claimed as trademarks. Where those designations appear in this book and Adams Media was
aware of a trademark claim, the designations have been printed with initial capital letters.

Photos taken by Kelly Jaggers
Interior illustrations © clipart.com

This book is available at quantity discounts for bulk purchases.
For information, please call 1-800-289-0963.

This book is dedicated to the most important women in my life: Carol, Lee, Ruby, and Wilda. You are loved.

Acknowledgments

First, I would like to thank my editors, Lisa and Katie, at Adams Media for all their support during this pie journey. You ladies have made this whole process easy, and I owe you both for making me look so good. Thank you for giving me a chance. I owe a tremendous debt to all the people who have taste-tested recipes for me. Thank you for your feedback, and for saving my waistline from all that pie. You are all troopers!

Special thanks go to my mother, Carol, for helping me when I was in a crunch for time by testing recipes. You have no idea how much that helped. I also need to thank my best friend, Jennifer, for your long-distance support. You may be across the pond, but you are always in my heart.

Finally, I want to thank my husband, Mark, for everything, but more specifically for his patience, understanding, and love.

Contents

Chapter 4
Fruits, Nuts, and Berries 69

Chapter 5
Tarts, Tartlets, and Rustic Pies . . . 99

PART 3
Savory Situations

Chapter 6

Dinner Pies 133

Chapter 7

Spicy, Salty, and Exotic Pies 165

INTRODUCTION

Pomegranate. Fresh figs. Sea salt.

Sounds delicious, right? These fresh ingredients are upscale, modern, and indulgent—and they're making an appearance in gourmet dishes across the world. But they're also showing up in the most unexpected places, like the pie plate in your kitchen.

Pie. The word evokes images of home, comfort, family, and everything that is wholesome and good. But a pie is only as good as the ingredients used to make it—and it's time to say goodbye to grandma's humble apple, cherry, or blueberry baked goods. Today's bakers are experimenting with exciting flavors, textures, and fillings to create a new breed of pie that is as sophisticated as it is comforting. So say hello to the new generation of *Not-So-Humble Pies.*

These new pies come in all shapes and sizes, and can be sweet or savory. Throughout this book, you'll find recipes that will tickle all of your taste buds—and are right for any and all upscale occasions. But when considering ingredients, remember that quality counts. For fruits and vegetables, try shopping at the local farmers' market, and discover what's in season where you live. You'll be amazed at the culinary treasures you'll walk away with; these fresh ingredients can range from locally harvested honey and free-range eggs to fresh herbs, locally roasted coffee, fresh flowers, and even freshly butchered meats. And if you're looking for exotic spices, cheeses, or anything else out of the ordinary, take a look at the gourmet shops in your area. Not only will the staff in these stores take the time to show you around and explain what they sell, they will be able to direct you to substitutions or other ingredients you may not have considered. Do not be afraid to ask questions and use your senses.

But while what goes in a pie is important, how you present your pie to your guests, family, and friends is important, too. In Part 1, you'll find recipes for upscale pie crusts and over-the-top toppings. You may not realize it, but you can take pie from homemade to high class with just a simple egg wash—a mixture of egg and a little water—which will give your pie a glistening finish, sanding sugars to make your pie sparkle, or fancy piping tubes that you can use to pipe detailed whipped cream or meringue designs. You can also play with chopped toasted nuts, fresh grated coconut, shaved chocolate, or even gold leaf, which you can use as a final flourish when you want a pie that is as pleasing to the eye as it is to the palate.

Above all else, pie is something to be shared and enjoyed, whether you're hosting a family dinner or a high-end function. Pie can be impressive or homey, but it shouldn't ever be boring. Take a chance, explore new flavors, experiment, and don't be afraid to let your pie take center stage. Because no matter how you choose to make it and share it, today's pie is anything but humble. Bon appétit!

PART 1

Not-So-Humble Beginnings

All-Butter Pie Crust

All-butter crusts have a lovely melt-in-the-mouth texture that makes them perfect for any type of upscale pie or tart. That said, butter can be tricky to work with since it melts at around 90°F. When making an all-butter pie crust, use very cold butter that is cut into ½" cubes; chilling the butter in the freezer for 10 minutes before rubbing it into the flour will make things a lot easier.

YIELDS 1 (9") CRUST

1¼ cups all-purpose flour
1 tablespoon sugar
½ teaspoon salt
8 tablespoons unsalted butter, cubed and chilled
3–4 tablespoons ice water

In a large bowl, sift together the flour, sugar, and salt.

Add the butter to the bowl; with your fingers, rub it into the flour until the mixture looks like coarse sand studded with pea-sized pieces of butter.

Add 2 tablespoons of water; mix until the dough forms a rough ball. Add more water, 1 tablespoon at a time, if needed.

Turn the dough out onto a lightly floured surface and form a disk. Wrap in plastic and chill for at least 30 minutes, or up to 3 days.

Remove the dough from the refrigerator for 10 minutes before rolling out. Roll out on a lightly floured surface to an ⅛" thick, 12" circle, turning the dough often to make sure it does not stick. Dust the surface with additional flour, if needed.

Fold the dough in half and place it into a 9" pie plate. Unfold and carefully press the dough into the pan. Use kitchen scissors or a paring knife to trim the dough to within 1" of the pan's edge.

Cover with plastic and chill until ready to bake. Covered, the crust will keep for up to three days in the refrigerator.

Pepper Jack Pastry Crust

To imbue your pies with a spicy kick, pair them with this festive pepper jack cheese–laced crust. This crust is delicious when used for savory pies, but think about using it for your favorite fruit pies, too. Apples, pears, apricots, cherries, and even peaches would pair beautifully with the earthy, spicy cheese in this crust.

YIELDS 1 (9") CRUST

1¼ cups all-purpose flour
½ teaspoon salt
¼ teaspoon paprika
½ cup butter, cubed and chilled
1 cup shredded pepper jack cheese
3–4 tablespoons ice water

In a large bowl, sift together the flour, salt, and paprika.

Add the chilled butter; rub into the flour mixture with your fingers until 30 percent of the fat is between pea and hazelnut sized, while the rest is blended in well.

Add the pepper jack cheese; mix until evenly incorporated.

Add 3 tablespoons of water; mix until the dough forms a rough ball. Add more water, 1 tablespoon at a time, as needed.

Turn the dough out onto a lightly floured surface and form the dough into a disk. Wrap in plastic and chill for at least 1 hour, or up to 3 days.

Remove the disk from the refrigerator for 10 minutes to warm up. Once warm, knead the dough 10 times on a well-floured surface. Roll out to an ⅛" thick, 12" circle, turning the dough often to make sure it does not stick. Dust the surface with additional flour, if needed.

Fold the dough in half and place it into a 9" pie plate. Unfold and carefully push the dough into the pan. Use kitchen scissors or a paring knife to trim the dough to within 1" of the pan's edge.

Cover with plastic and place in the refrigerator to chill until ready to bake. Covered, the crust will keep for up to three days in the refrigerator.

Almond Pastry Crust

The sweet nutty flavor of almonds gives this crust an extra pop of flavor and, since almonds complement so many flavors, this recipe can add a nuanced flavor to your next pie. Ground almonds can be purchased at most natural food stores and in the gluten-free section of some grocery stores, but if you can't find them you can make them very easily at home. Grind whole, blanched almonds in a food processor until they are the texture of coarse sand.

YIELD 1 (9") CRUST

1 cup plus 2 tablespoons all-purpose flour

¼ cup ground almonds

2 tablespoons sugar

½ teaspoon salt

4 tablespoons butter, cubed and chilled

4 tablespoons vegetable shortening, chilled

¼ teaspoon almond extract

2–4 tablespoons ice water

In a large bowl, whisk together the flour, almonds, sugar, and salt.

Add the butter and shortening; with your fingers, rub it into the flour until the mixture looks like coarse sand studded with pea-sized pieces of butter.

Add the almond extract and 2 tablespoons of water; mix until the dough forms a rough ball. Add more water, 1 tablespoon at a time, if needed.

Turn the dough out onto a lightly floured surface and form a disk. Wrap in plastic and chill for at least 30 minutes, or up to 3 days.

Remove the dough from the refrigerator for 10 minutes to warm up. Roll out on a lightly floured surface to an ⅛" thick, 12" circle, turning the dough often to make sure it does not stick. Dust the surface with additional flour, if needed.

Fold the dough in half and place it into a 9" pie plate. Unfold and carefully press the dough into the pan. Use kitchen scissors or a paring knife to trim the dough to within 1" of the pan's edge.

Cover with plastic and chill until ready to bake. Covered, the crust will keep for up to three days in the refrigerator.

Lard Crust

Lard, widely used in baking and cooking until vegetable shortening came onto the market, produces pie crusts that have a refined flavor and texture. Compared to shortening and butter, lard offers a clean flavor, retains a melt-in-the-mouth richness on your palate, and just crisps up beautifully once baked. Because lard melts at a higher temperature than butter—and is more forgiving to work with—this crust allows the filling in your pie to shine.

YIELDS 1 (9") CRUST

1¼ cups all-purpose flour
½ teaspoon salt
½ cup lard, chilled
1 egg yolk
1 teaspoon white distilled vinegar
2 tablespoons ice water

In a large bowl, sift together the flour and salt.

Add the lard; with your fingers, rub it into the flour until the mixture looks like coarse sand studded with pea-sized pieces of fat.

In a separate bowl, whisk together the egg yolk, vinegar, and water.

Add 2 tablespoons of the liquid to the dry ingredients; mix until the dough forms a rough ball. Add more liquid, 1 tablespoon at a time, if needed.

Turn the dough out onto a lightly floured surface and form a disk. Wrap in plastic and chill for at least 30 minutes, or up to 3 days.

Remove the dough from the refrigerator for 10 minutes to warm up. Roll out on a lightly floured surface to an ⅛" thick, 12" circle, turning the dough often to make sure it does not stick. Dust the surface with additional flour, if needed.

Fold the dough in half and place it into a 9" pie plate. Unfold and carefully press the dough into the pan. Use kitchen scissors or a paring knife to trim the dough to within 1" of the pan's edge.

Cover with plastic and chill until ready to bake. Covered, the crust will keep for up to three days in the refrigerator.

Traditional Graham Cracker Crust

This cookie crust brings a lot to the table. Not only does it taste fantastic, it offers a crispy, crumbly texture and a rustic appeal that makes even an upscale soiree feel like home. Use cookie crusts for pies that are not baked in the oven—like cream pies—or with fruit fillings that are cooked on the stovetop.

YIELDS 1 (9") CRUST

1⅓ cups graham cracker crumbs
3 tablespoons sugar
6 tablespoons unsalted butter, melted

Preheat the oven to 350°F.

In a medium bowl, combine the graham cracker crumbs, sugar, and butter until well combined. Press the mixture evenly into a 9" pie pan.

Bake for 10–12 minutes, or until the crust is golden brown and the center is firm when pressed lightly. Cool completely before filling.

Pretzel Crust

Salty and crunchy, a pretzel crust is an easy way to give your favorite pie an unexpected twist. The salty crunch of pretzels helps spark the sweetness of the filling, and the naturally hearty flavor of pretzels adds a mouthwatering layer of flavor to your pie. But be careful: Large pieces of pretzel will make the crust fragile and it will fall apart when sliced. Use a food processor to process the pretzels until they have the texture of sand.

YIELDS 1 (9") CRUST

1¼ cups finely crushed pretzels

¼ cup sugar

¼ cup unsalted butter, melted

Preheat the oven to 350°F.

In a medium bowl, combine the pretzel crumbs, sugar, and butter until well combined. Press the mixture evenly into a 9" pie pan.

Bake for 10–12 minutes, or until the crust is golden brown and the center is firm when pressed lightly. Cool completely before filling.

Short Crust for Tarts

This recipe produces a sturdy dough that is very easy to work with. The pastry holds its shape well while baking, unmolds easily from the tart pan, and produces clean, pretty slices. This crust, similar in texture and flavor to a shortbread cookie, is particularly nice when combined with fresh fruit or custards.

YIELDS 1 (9") CRUST

¼ cup sugar

1 stick unsalted butter, slightly softened

1 egg

½ teaspoon vanilla

1⅓ cups all-purpose flour

Cream together the sugar and butter until just combined.

Add in the egg yolk and vanilla; mix until incorporated.

Add in the flour; mix until the dough is smooth. Wrap in plastic and chill for 1 hour, or up to 3 days.

Remove the dough from the refrigerator for 10 minutes to warm up. Roll out on a lightly floured surface to an ⅛" thick, 12" circle, turning the dough often to make sure it does not stick. Dust the surface with additional flour, if needed.

Roll the dough around the rolling pin and unroll it into a 10" tart pan. Carefully press the dough into the pan. Press your fingers against the rim of the pan to trim the dough.

Cover with plastic and chill until ready to bake. Covered, the crust will keep for up to three days in the refrigerator.

Lemon and Lavender Short Crust Pastry

The fresh lemon and lavender used in this recipe make this delicately flavored crust unforgettably upscale. Use this crust when making fresh fruit tarts to emphasize the flavors of the berries. This base is also lovely with a simple vanilla custard or some creamy lemon curd. Orange and lime zest can also be used here, so don't be afraid to customize your crust and make it your own.

YIELDS 1 (9") CRUST

¼ cup packed light brown sugar

1 stick unsalted butter, slightly softened

1 egg

1 teaspoon fresh lemon zest

½ teaspoon vanilla

1⅓ cups all-purpose flour

¼ teaspoon dried culinary lavender, crushed

¼ teaspoon salt

Cream together the sugar and butter until just combined.

Add in the egg, lemon zest, and vanilla; mix until incorporated.

Add in the flour, lavender, and salt; mix until the dough is smooth. If needed, add additional flour, 1 tablespoon at a time, if the dough is too sticky. Wrap in plastic and chill for 1 hour, or up to three days.

Remove the dough from the refrigerator for 10 minutes to warm up. Roll out on a lightly floured surface to an ⅛" thick, 12" circle, turning the dough often to make sure it does not stick. Dust the surface with additional flour, if needed.

Roll the dough around the rolling pin and unroll it into a 10" tart pan. Carefully press the dough into the pan. Press your fingers against the rim of the pan to trim the dough.

Cover with plastic and chill until ready to bake. Covered, the crust will keep for up to three days in the refrigerator.

Spicy Cheddar Crust

Cheddar cheese has a sharp, rich flavor and an enticing aroma. Here it's combined with a hint of spicy cayenne pepper to create a crust with a flavor similar to the cheese straw, a staple of the South. This crust is best when filled with apple, pear, or even peach fillings where the sharp cheese can play off the fragrant fruit.

YIELDS 2 (9") CRUSTS

2½ cups all-purpose flour

1 teaspoon salt

¼ teaspoon cayenne pepper

1 cup (2 sticks) unsalted butter, cubed and chilled

2 cups shredded sharp Cheddar cheese

6–8 tablespoons ice water

In a large bowl, sift together the flour, salt, and cayenne pepper. Add the chilled butter; rub into the flour mixture with your fingers until 30 percent of the fat is between pea and hazelnut sized, while the rest is blended in well. Add the Cheddar cheese and mix until evenly incorporated.

Add 3 tablespoons of water and mix until the dough forms a rough ball. Add more water, 1 tablespoon at a time, as needed.

Turn the dough out onto a lightly floured surface. Divide the dough in half. Form each half into a disk. Wrap in plastic and chill for at least 1 hour, or up to 3 days.

Remove one of the disks from the refrigerator for 10 minutes to warm up. Once warm, knead the dough 10 times on a well-floured surface. Roll out to an ⅛" thick, 12" circle, turning the dough often to make sure it does not stick. Dust the surface with additional flour, if needed.

Fold the dough in half and place it into a 9" pie plate. Unfold and carefully push the dough into the pan. Use kitchen scissors or a paring knife to trim the dough to within ½" of the pan's edge. Cover with plastic and place in the refrigerator to chill.

Remove the second disk of dough from the refrigerator for 10 minutes to warm up. Roll out on a lightly floured surface to an ⅛" thick, 12" circle, turning the dough often to make sure it does not stick. Dust the surface with additional flour, if needed.

Place the crust on a baking sheet and chill for 30 minutes before use.

Graham Pecan Crust

Both buttery and nutty, pecans add not only a rich, decadent flavor but a pleasant, chewy texture to this crisp crust. Not a fan of pecans? You can use any ground nuts you like here. Hazelnuts, almonds, walnuts, and even macadamia nuts are excellent substitutes. You can also substitute chocolate wafer cookies for the graham crackers. In fact, if you added ground hazelnuts you would have a crust that mimicked in flavor the popular chocolate hazelnut spread.

YIELDS 1 (9") CRUST

1 cup plus 2 tablespoons graham cracker crumbs
⅓ cup ground pecans
¼ teaspoon cinnamon
¼ cup sugar
6 tablespoons unsalted butter, melted

Preheat the oven to 350°F.

In a medium bowl, combine the graham cracker crumbs, ground pecans, cinnamon, sugar, and butter until well combined. Press the mixture evenly into a 9" pie pan.

Bake for 10–12 minutes, or until the crust is golden brown and the center is firm when pressed lightly. Cool completely before filling.

Ginger Snap Crust

When you are making a pie with a spicy filling, think about adding some warm spice to your crust, too. This causes the warm flavor profile of the spices to carry through your entire dish. You will want to use crunchy ginger snaps for this crust. The soft kind—while a pleasure to eat—are too soggy to form a solid base. If you have any left-over crispy gingerbread cookies, you can also use those here.

YIELDS 1 (9") CRUST

⅔ cup graham cracker crumbs

⅔ cup gingersnap crumbs

2 tablespoons sugar

6 tablespoons unsalted butter, melted

Preheat the oven to 350°F.

In a medium bowl, combine the graham cracker crumbs, gingersnap crumbs, sugar, and butter until well combined. Press the mixture evenly into a 9" pie pan.

Bake for 10-12 minutes, or until the crust is golden brown and the center is firm when pressed lightly. Cool completely before filling.

Chocolate Cookie Crust

Want to take the chocolate flavor of your pie to the next level? Then this is the crust for you! If you are feeling particularly exotic, you can add even more flavor by adding a couple of tablespoons of toasted coconut, a teaspoon of instant coffee, or ¼ teaspoon of cinnamon to the cookie crumbs.

YIELDS 1 (9") CRUST

1⅓ cups chocolate wafer cookie crumbs

2 tablespoons sugar

6 tablespoons unsalted butter, melted

Preheat the oven to 350°F.

In a medium bowl, combine the cookie crumbs, sugar, and butter until well combined. Press the mixture evenly into a 9" pie pan.

Bake for 10–12 minutes, or until the crust is firm in the center when pressed lightly. Cool completely before filling.

Blitz Puff Pastry

Traditional puff pastry can be quite tricky and time consuming to make: a block of cold butter is incorporated into dough, which is then repeatedly rolled out, folded, and chilled to create thousands of flaky layers. It can take a day, or more, to make this intricate pastry properly. This recipe makes a puff pastry with a lot of delicate, flaky layers, but from start to finish this takes less than an hour. Your guests will think you spent hours in the kitchen perfecting this impressive puff—and you don't have to tell them otherwise!

SERVES 8

1⅓ cups all-purpose flour

1 tablespoon sugar

¼ teaspoon salt

1½ sticks unsalted butter, cut into 1" pieces and chilled

6 tablespoons ice water

In a large bowl, combine the flour, sugar, and salt; mix well.

Add the chilled butter; blend it into the flour mixture with your fingers until 10 percent of the fat is blended in well, leaving the rest as very large chunks, between hazelnut and pecan size.

Add the water a little at a time, and mix the dough with a spatula until it just hangs together. It will look very shaggy.

Turn the dough out onto a well-floured surface. Shape the dough into a rectangle; roll out to ½" thick. Dust the top with additional flour if the butter is too soft, but do not add too much.

Use a bench scraper or a large spatula to fold the dough into itself in thirds, similar to folding a letter. It will be crumbly.

Turn the dough 90° and square off the edges. Roll into a rectangle that's ½" thick. Brush off any excess flour; fold in thirds.

Repeat this process 2 more times; wrap in plastic and chill for 30 minutes.

Remove from the refrigerator and allow to stand for 10 minutes.

Roll the dough out into a ½" thick rectangle, dust off any excess flour as you fold, then fold

the 2 shorter sides into the center and then in half at the seam, like a book.

Roll out the dough to ½" thick; wrap in plastic and chill for 1 hour before use.

Cornmeal Tart Crust

Looking for a tart crust with a little something more? The magic ingredient in this recipe is cornmeal, which adds an interesting texture and savory flavor and is perfect when paired with bold-flavored fillings. Use a finely ground cornmeal for this recipe. While stone-ground cornmeal has a beautiful texture and flavor, it can be a little overwhelming for this recipe because of its rustic coarseness. A finer ground cornmeal will provide all the toothsome quality of cornmeal, all the earthy flavor, but it will not distract from the filling it houses.

YIELDS 1 (10") TART

1 cup all-purpose flour

¼ cup yellow cornmeal

¼ teaspoon salt

⅓ cup unsalted butter, room temperature

¼ cup sugar

1 egg

2 tablespoons water

In a medium bowl, combine the flour, cornmeal, and salt until thoroughly blended.

In a separate bowl, whisk together the butter and sugar until lightened in color. Whisk in the egg.

Add dry ingredients to the butter mixture; stir until just combined.

Add the water; continue to mix until the dough starts to clump together.

On a well-floured surface, flatten the dough into a disk; wrap in plastic and refrigerate for 30 minutes.

Remove the dough from the refrigerator for 10 minutes to warm up. Roll out on a lightly floured surface to an ⅛" thick, 12" circle, turning the dough often to make sure it does not stick. Dust the surface with additional flour, if needed.

Fold the dough in half and place it into a 10" tart pan with 1" sides. Unfold and carefully press the dough into the pan. Press the dough against the edge of the pan to trim.

Cover with plastic and chill until ready to bake. Covered, the crust will keep for up to three days in the refrigerator.

Parmesan Pastry Crust

Parmesan cheese is a hard Italian cow's milk cheese prized for its savory flavor—and its inclusion in this crust will take the sophistication of your pie to a whole new level. When it comes to Parmesan, it is wise to invest a little in the real thing. Avoid the shelf-stable canisters of grated cheese next to the dry pasta and opt instead for blocks of freshly cut cheese found in the deli. Fresh Parmesan is a little more expensive, but it's well worth it; you'll be rewarded with a stronger, saltier flavor and a creamier aroma.

YIELDS 1 (10") TART

1⅔ cups all-purpose flour

¼ teaspoon baking powder

½ teaspoon salt

2 ounces grated Parmesan cheese

1 stick unsalted butter, cubed and chilled

2 tablespoons ice water

1 teaspoon white vinegar

In a large bowl, whisk together the flour, baking powder, salt, and cheese.

Add the chilled butter; rub it into the flour mixture with your fingers until 30 percent of the fat is pea sized, while the rest is blended in well.

Add the water and vinegar; mix until the dough forms a rough ball. Add more water, a few drops at a time, if needed.

Turn the dough out onto a lightly floured surface and form a disk. Wrap in plastic and chill for at least 30 minutes, or up to 3 days.

Remove the dough from the refrigerator for 10 minutes to warm up. Roll out on a lightly floured surface to an ⅛" thick, 11" circle, turning the dough often to make sure it does not stick. Dust the surface with additional flour, if needed.

Fold the dough in half and place it into a 9" tart pan with 1" sides. Unfold and carefully press the dough into the pan. Press the dough against the edge of the pan to trim.

Cover with plastic and chill until ready to bake. Covered, the crust will keep for up to three days in the refrigerator.

Brown Butter–Graham Cracker Tart Crust

The subtle, nutty, buttery flavor of the brown butter used in this crust works well in dishes that have warm spices or caramel. When butter browns, some of the water evaporates while the butter solids separate and sink to the bottom of the pot, where they gently toast. Keep your eye on your butter as you brown it. It can go from toasty and delicious to burned in seconds.

YIELDS 1 (10") TART

6 tablespoons unsalted butter

1¾ cups graham cracker crumbs

⅓ cup packed light brown sugar

Preheat the oven to 350°F.

In a small saucepan over medium-low heat, add the butter; cook until it is nut brown, about 10 minutes, stirring constantly to prevent hot spots. Cool the butter to room temperature.

In a medium bowl, combine the graham cracker crumbs, sugar, and butter until well combined. Press the mixture evenly into a 10" tart pan.

Bake for 10–12 minutes, or until the crust is golden brown and the center is firm when pressed lightly. Cool completely before filling.

Chapter 2

Toppings

To truly make a pie that's sophisticated, upscale, and absolutely beautiful, you need to gild the lily with something decadent, like salted caramel, spiked whipped cream, or spiced chocolate. Some toppings are simply synonymous with specific pies: Lemon pie is not the same without the golden-peaked meringue. Chocolate cream pie is just chocolate pudding in a cookie crust until you spread on the whipped cream. Apple crumble pie is not the same without that crisp, buttery, golden brown crumble topping. But here, you'll learn how to take these toppings from simple to sophisticated in no time flat. So, forget the lattice on that cherry pie, substitute an earthy oat topping. Top your strawberry tart with an airy yet slightly toasty meringue piped into an elaborate design. The options are only limited by your imagination.

Butter Crumble

Something as simple as butter, flour, sugar, and salt can create an absolutely show-stopping pie topping. This very simple crumble is a wonderful topping for fruit pies, and you can doll it up with spices such as ¼ teaspoon of cinnamon or even a tablespoon of cocoa powder.

YIELDS ENOUGH CRUMBLE FOR 1 (9") PIE

½ cup all-purpose flour

½ cup sugar

¼ teaspoon salt

⅓ cup unsalted butter, cubed and chilled

In a bowl, blend the flour, sugar, and salt.

Using your fingers, rub in the butter until the mixture resembles coarse sand.

Chill the crumble for 30 minutes before use.

Oat Crumble

This oat crumble is very cozy and reassuringly rustic. Once the crumble has finished baking, the oats will have toasted and absorbed some of the butter, making them slightly crisp on the top but tender and soft underneath.

YIELDS ENOUGH CRUMBLE FOR 1 (9") PIE

¼ cup all-purpose flour

¼ cup rolled oats

¼ teaspoon cinnamon

½ cup sugar

¼ teaspoon salt

⅓ cup unsalted butter, cubed and chilled

In a bowl, blend the flour, oats, cinnamon, sugar, and salt.

Using your fingers, rub in the butter until the mixture resembles coarse sand.

Chill the crumble for 30 minutes before use.

Pecan Streusel

Hearty, juicy fruit and toasty pecans are a combination that is hard to beat. In general, streusel topping and fruit pies make a fine match, but if you're really looking to impress your guests with this not-so-humble pie topping, be brave and opt for a combination of pecans, almonds, and walnuts or go wild and grind up some macadamia nuts or cashews!

YIELDS ENOUGH CRUMBLE FOR 1 (9") PIE

¼ cup firmly packed light brown sugar

¼ cup sugar

½ cup all-purpose flour

¼ cup unsalted butter, cubed and chilled

⅓ cup chopped pecans

In a bowl, blend the brown sugar, sugar, and flour.

Using your fingers, rub in the butter until the mixture resembles coarse sand. Add the pecans; mix well.

Chill for 30 minutes before use.

Cinnamon Streusel Topping

Rather than topping a double-crusted pie with another layer of pastry, substitute a streusel topping instead. The baking time stays the same, and a streusel topping is a fantastic time saver. But, even better, this topping looks more difficult to make than a regular pie crust, and this Cinnamon Streusel Topping will make your pie the talk of the town.

YIELDS ENOUGH CRUMBLE FOR 1 (9") PIE

½ cup all-purpose flour

½ cup packed light brown sugar

½ teaspoon cinnamon

¼ teaspoon salt

⅓ cup unsalted butter, cubed and chilled

In a bowl, blend the flour, brown sugar, cinnamon, and salt.

Using your fingers, rub in the butter until the mixture resembles coarse sand.

Chill the crumble for 30 minutes before use.

Foolproof Meringue

There are not many things more impressive than a pie topped with a toasty, billowing cloud of perfectly whipped meringue. Sadly, meringues have a reputation for being rather tricky to prepare, but this recipe takes all the fear out of meringue making. This topping is exceptional on cream and custard pies because the light texture contrasts nicely against the thick custard filling. This is also lovely on fruit fillings if you're looking for a change of pace.

SERVES 8

1 tablespoon cornstarch

⅓ cup cold water

4 egg whites, room temperature

1 pinch cream of tartar

6 tablespoons superfine sugar

1 teaspoon vanilla

Whisk the cornstarch into the water until smooth. Pour the mixture into a small pot; cook over medium heat, stirring constantly, until the starch thickens, about 5 minutes. Set aside to cool.

In a large bowl, add the egg whites and cream of tartar. Beat the egg whites on low speed until they become foamy, about 2 minutes. (This gives the whites a good base to build on.)

Increase the speed to medium and beat until the egg whites are just starting to increase in volume, about 1 minute, Add the sugar 1 tablespoon at a time (if you add the sugar too fast it may clump) along with the vanilla, and beat until the mixture forms soft peaks, about 1 minute.

Continue beating the egg whites; add cornstarch mixture 1 tablespoon at a time. Beat until the mixture forms firm peaks, about 2 minutes.

Immediately spread over pie filling and bake.

Sour Cream Topping

Say goodbye to modest fruit tarts! This rich, sweet, and tangy topping takes your tarts over the top, and it pairs really well with peaches, plums, and apricots! For an extra flavor bump, add a little nutmeg, mace, or cardamom.

SERVES 8

1 cup sour cream

2 tablespoons sugar, or more to taste

1 teaspoon vanilla or vanilla bean paste

Mix the sour cream, sugar, and vanilla together until smooth. Chill 1 hour before serving.

Stabilized Whipped Cream

Whipped cream is a lovely, deceptively simple way to dress up a pie, but if you don't use it right away it can deflate and become watery. To prevent this, all you have to do is stabilize the whipped cream with a little plain gelatin. Be sure to bloom, or soften, the gelatin thoroughly for the maximum holding power.

SERVES 8

½ teaspoon powdered gelatin

1½ teaspoons cold water

1 cup heavy whipping cream, cold

3 tablespoons powdered sugar

1 teaspoon vanilla

In a small bowl, mix the powdered gelatin with the cold water. Let stand 10 minutes, then melt in the microwave for 10 seconds. Allow to cool for 5 minutes, or until cool to the touch.

In a medium mixing bowl, add the cream, powdered sugar, and vanilla. Whip on medium-high speed in a stand mixer or with a hand mixer until it starts to thicken, about 1 minute.

Slowly pour in the cooled gelatin; whip until the cream forms medium peaks, about 1 minute.

Use immediately, or cover with plastic and store in the refrigerator for up to 3 days.

Spiked Whipped Cream

People of all ages will love your not-so-humble pies, but sometimes you want a pie that's all grown up, and this spirited whipped cream does the job! It is not loaded with alcohol—a little goes a long way—but it packs a distinct kick. Try this topping around the holidays made with spiced rum and a little nutmeg grated over the top.

SERVES 8

1 cup heavy whipping cream, cold

3 tablespoons powdered sugar

½ teaspoon vanilla

2 tablespoons bourbon, rum, or brandy

In a medium bowl, add the cream, powdered sugar, and vanilla.

Whip on medium-high speed in a stand mixer or with a hand mixer until it starts to thicken, about 1 minute.

Increase the speed to high; beat until soft peaks form, about 1 minute.

Reduce the speed to medium; slowly add the liquor. Continue to whip until medium peaks form, about 1 minute. Use immediately.

Biscuit Topping

This biscuit topping is commonly found on top of traditional fruit cobblers, but you can use it to make your pies even more amazing. This topping actually gave cobblers their name, in fact, because the baked biscuits look like cobble stones. If you want to make this topping even more sophisticated, you can use chilled brown butter in this topping in place of the regular butter on the ingredients list to get a deeper flavor.

YIELDS ENOUGH TO TOP 1 (9") PIE

1 cup all-purpose flour

1 tablespoon sugar

1 teaspoon baking powder

½ teaspoon salt

1 stick unsalted butter, cubed and chilled

¼ cup buttermilk

In a medium bowl, combine the flour, sugar, baking powder, and salt.

Add the cold butter; using your fingers, rub it in until it is the size of peas.

Add the buttermilk; using a spatula, stir until it is just combined. Do not overmix.

Using a disher or 2 spoons, scoop the dough by rounded tablespoons into the pie.

Salted Caramel Sauce

Thick, creamy, and agreeably salty, this sauce makes an elegant addition to most pies. Good sea salt is key to this recipe as it adds a mineral-rich saltiness without being overpowering or sharp like table or kosher salt would be. This sauce is not just for pies, however; it's also delicious when poured over cake, ice cream, or even when used as a dipping sauce for fresh fruit and cookies. Any leftover sauce should be kept in an airtight container in the refrigerator. Just allow the caramel to come to room temperature before serving.

YIELDS 1½ CUPS

1 cup sugar

2 tablespoons water

2 tablespoons light corn syrup

¾ cup heavy cream

4 tablespoons unsalted butter

1½ teaspoons sea salt, crushed

In a medium saucepan with deep sides over medium-high heat, combine the sugar, water, and corn syrup. Brush down the sides of the pan with a wet pastry brush until it begins to bubble.

Bring the mixture to a full boil and cook until it becomes dark amber in color and smells like caramel, about 6 minutes.

Remove the saucepan from the heat; carefully whisk in the cream, butter, and salt.

Allow the caramel to cool to room temperature before serving.

Spiced Chocolate Sauce

Sweet citrus, aromatic vanilla, and warm cinnamon make this chocolate sauce a flavorful and decadent treat to drizzle over fresh cut slices of pie. The warm flavors of the orange, honey, and spice give this sauce a seasonal appeal, so consider using it as a dramatic counterpart to a nut or pumpkin pie around the holidays. If you want to give this sauce a kick add a little chipotle or cayenne pepper for a spicy finish.

YIELDS 1½ CUPS

1½ cups heavy cream

1 tablespoon orange zest

1 cinnamon stick

1 vanilla bean, split and seeds scraped out

1 tablespoon honey

½ cup semisweet chocolate, chopped

In a medium saucepan over medium heat, combine the cream, orange zest, cinnamon stick, vanilla bean with seeds, and honey; cook until the cream just begins to boil.

Remove from the heat and strain the cream into a medium bowl.

Add the chopped chocolate; let it stand for 1 minute, then whisk until smooth. Serve warm.

Chocolate–Peanut Butter Fudge Sauce

Chocolate and peanut butter is a classic combination and this recipe provides the perfect blend of both. This glossy sauce's lush texture and rich flavor makes it the perfect thing to pour over a slice of whipped cream–topped cream pie. It also makes a self-indulgent stand-in for regular chocolate syrup on an ice cream sundae.

YIELDS 1½ CUPS

¾ cup heavy cream

½ cup semisweet chocolate, chopped

½ cup creamy peanut butter

2 tablespoons honey

In a medium saucepan combine the cream, chocolate, peanut butter, and honey. Cook over medium-low heat until the chocolate is completely melted and the mixture is smooth. Serve warm.

PART 2

Sweet~as~
Can~Be

With flavors ranging from rustic and comforting to polished and sophisticated, nothing provides a sweeter ending to an everyday meal at home or a sophisticated special celebration than pie. Pies make a wonderful dessert, but they are also a unique way of giving comfort, sharing a little sweet pleasure, and showing people how much you care. In this section, you'll find recipes for wonderfully distinctive sweet pies and tarts that are full of rich flavors ranging from tea and lavender to saffron and exotic spices. There are even tarts laced with bourbon, brandy, and rum. Use these recipes to discover the epicurean world of pies that are sweet as can be!

Chapter 3

Creams, Custards, and Chiffons

If you like your pies smooth and luscious, then the cream, custard, and chiffon pies in this chapter are for you. Here, you'll find recipes for marvelously silky cream pies, rich custard pies, and chiffon pies so light they whisper across your tongue. But today's recipes go beyond the everyday and into the extraordinary with beautiful textures and trendy, unique ingredients like pomegranate, maple syrup, cardamom, saffron, and limoncello. So, say goodbye to plain old vanilla, and get ready for a delicious adventure!

Pomegranate Cream Cheese Pie

SERVES 8

2 cups pomegranate juice

6 ounces cream cheese, softened

1 cup powdered sugar

1 cup heavy cream

½ teaspoon vanilla

1 (9") Traditional Graham Cracker Crust (see Chapter 1), baked and cooled

½ cup fresh pomegranate seeds, for garnish

If you're looking for a not-so-humble ingredient to elevate a humble pie, look no further than the pomegranate. This fruit is native to the Middle East and is a common ingredient in Persian and Indian cooking. Pomegranate juice is sweet yet tangy, and in this pie it is concentrated down into a thick syrup that adds maximum flavor while keeping your pie filling thick and rich. Look for pomegranate juice with no added sugar for the best flavor.

In a medium saucepan over medium heat, add the pomegranate juice; bring to a simmer. Cook, stirring occasionally, until reduced to ¼ cup, about 20 minutes. Cool to room temperature.

In a large bowl, cream together the pomegranate syrup, cream cheese, and powdered sugar and mix until smooth, then set aside.

In a separate bowl, whip the cream with the vanilla until it forms medium peaks, about 1½ minutes.

Fold the cream into the pomegranate mixture until no streaks of cream remain.

Pour the mixture into the Traditional Graham Cracker Crust and garnish with the pomegranate seeds. Chill for 4 hours before serving.

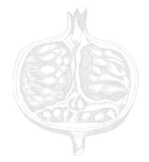

Chocolate Acai Chiffon Pie

SERVES 8

1 tablespoon unflavored powdered gelatin

2 tablespoons cold water

¼ cup acai berry juice

4 egg yolks

1 cup sugar, divided

3 ounces bittersweet chocolate, melted and cooled

4 egg whites

¼ teaspoon salt

1 teaspoon vanilla

1 (9") Chocolate Cookie Crust (see Chapter 1), baked and cooled

1 recipe Stabilized Whipped Cream (see Chapter 2)

This pie contains acai berry juice and dark chocolate, both of which are loaded with flavonoids, powerful antioxidants that may help prevent cardiovascular disease and cancer. Acai fruit, which are harvested from a palm tree that is common to South America, are actually drupes, not berries, meaning they have a pit surrounded by a fruit covering.

In a small bowl, combine the gelatin and the water. Allow to stand until completely bloomed, about 10 minutes.

In a medium saucepan over medium heat, add the acai juice and bring to a simmer. Cook, stirring occasionally, until reduced to ¼ cup, about 20 minutes. Cool to room temperature.

In a double boiler, combine the egg yolks with ½ cup of the sugar and whisk until thickened, about 10 minutes.

Remove from the heat and add the bloomed gelatin, acai syrup, and melted chocolate. Whisk until completely dissolved. Allow to cool until the mixture begins to thicken.

In a large bowl, whip the egg whites with the salt and vanilla until they are very frothy. Gradually add in the remaining sugar, beating constantly, until the whites form medium peaks, about 1½ minutes.

Working in thirds, fold the egg whites into the chocolate mixture, making sure no large streaks of egg white remain.

Pour the mixture into the Chocolate Cookie Crust; cover with cling film and chill until firm, about 4 hours.

Once chilled, prepare the Stabilized Whipped Cream. Top the pie and chill for 30 minutes before serving.

Cantaloupe Cream Pie

SERVES 8

1 cup cantaloupe, peeled, seeded, and cubed

2 cups sugar

⅓ cup cornstarch

3 egg yolks

2 cups whole milk

1 teaspoon vanilla

2 tablespoons butter

1 (9") Traditional Graham Cracker Crust (see Chapter 1), baked and cooled

1 recipe Stabilized Whipped Cream (see Chapter 2)

Cantaloupe is available all year long, but for the freshest flavor, check out your local markets from June to August, when this delicious melon is in season. Remember to thoroughly wash your cantaloupe before cutting to avoid contaminating the flesh with harmful bacteria, and never keep a cut cantaloupe for longer than 3 days in the refrigerator.

In a blender, purée the cantaloupe until smooth, about 2 minutes.

In a medium saucepan, combine the purée, sugar, cornstarch, egg yolks, and milk. Cook over medium heat, whisking constantly, until it simmers and thickens, about 6 minutes.

Remove from the heat and add the vanilla and butter. Stir until melted.

Pour the custard directly into the Traditional Graham Cracker Crust. Cover the custard with a layer of cling film and chill overnight.

Once chilled, prepare the Stabilized Whipped Cream and spread over the pie. Chill for 30 minutes before serving.

Mango Chiffon Pie

SERVES 8

2 ripe mangos

¼ cup water

1 tablespoon powdered gelatin

5 eggs, separated

2 tablespoons lime juice

½ cup sugar, divided

1 teaspoon lime zest

¼ teaspoon salt

1 (9") Traditional Graham Cracker Crust (see Chapter 1), baked and cooled

1 recipe Stabilized Whipped Cream (see Chapter 2)

The mango originates from India, but today the fruit is grown year round across the globe in countries with tropical, frost-free climates. Fruity and a little exotic, mango gives this light chiffon filling a striking flavor and its bold, golden color also gives this pie a striking visual impact. If fresh mango is unavailable, you can use frozen mango for this pie. Simply thaw the fruit and drain off any liquid before puréeing.

Peel and slice the mango into the work bowl of a blender; purée until very smooth, about 3 minutes. This should yield 1½ cups of purée.

In a small bowl, combine the water and gelatin; allow to stand for 10 minutes.

In a double boiler, combine the egg yolks, lime juice, ¼ cup sugar, lime zest, salt, and mango purée. Cook, whisking constantly, until thickened, about 5 minutes.

Remove from the heat; add the bloomed gelatin. Whisk until dissolved. Allow to cool until it thickens.

In a large bowl, whip the egg whites with the salt until they are very frothy, about 30 seconds.

Gradually add in the remaining sugar, beating constantly, until the whites form medium peaks, about 1 minute.

Working in thirds, fold the egg whites into the mango mixture, making sure no large streaks of egg white remain.

Pour the mixture into the Traditional Graham Cracker Crust and chill until firm, about 4 hours.

Once chilled, prepare the Stabilized Whipped Cream and top the pie. Chill for 30 minutes before serving.

Cookies and Cream Mousse Pie

SERVES 8

1¼ cups milk

¼ cup heavy cream

½ cup sugar

3 tablespoons cornstarch

2 egg yolks

¼ teaspoon salt

1 tablespoon butter

2 teaspoons vanilla

½ teaspoon powdered gelatin

1 tablespoon cold water

1 cup heavy whipping cream

3 tablespoons powdered sugar

1 teaspoon vanilla

¾ cup crushed chocolate sandwich cookies

1 Chocolate Cookie Crust (see Chapter 1), baked and cooled

Who doesn't love good, old-fashioned chocolate sandwich cookies— especially when they're mixed into ice cream or dunked into chilly glasses of milk? Add a chocolate-y layer of playful sophistication to this kids' snack by mixing crushed chocolate sandwich cookies into a creamy vanilla mousse pie. You can also use vanilla or even peanut butter sandwich cookies in this pie, or a combination of all three!

In a medium saucepan, combine the milk, cream, sugar, cornstarch, egg yolks, and salt and whisk until smooth. Cook over medium heat, stirring constantly, until it begins to simmer and thicken, about 8 minutes.

Remove from the heat and add the butter and vanilla. Stir until melted.

Pour through a strainer into a separate bowl. Place a layer of cling film directly on the custard and chill for 1 hour.

In a small bowl, mix the powdered gelatin with the cold water. Let stand 10 minutes, then melt in the microwave for 10 seconds. Allow to cool for 5 minutes, or until cool to the touch.

In a medium bowl, add the cream, powdered sugar, and vanilla, and using a hand mixer, whip on medium-high speed until it starts to thicken, about 1 minute.

Slowly pour in the cooled gelatin; whip until the cream forms medium peaks, about 1 minute. Cover and chill for 30 minutes.

Add ½ of the whipped cream and ½ cup of the crushed cookies to the vanilla mixture; gently fold to incorporate.

Pour into the Chocolate Cookie Crust and garnish the top with the remaining whipped cream and crushed cookies. Chill for 4 hours before serving.

Brandied Sweet Potato Pie

SERVES 8

3 medium sweet potatoes, peeled and cut into 1" pieces

¾ cup packed light brown sugar

1 teaspoon cinnamon

¼ teaspoon salt

¼ teaspoon allspice

⅛ teaspoon fresh-grated nutmeg

2 tablespoons brandy

2 eggs

12 ounces evaporated milk

1 (9") Mealy Pie Crust (see Chapter 1), unbaked

Brandy was initially used as a way to preserve wine for long sea voyages. Wine was distilled, concentrating it to save space, and stored in wood casks. Once the brandy reached its destination, the intention was to add back the water lost in the distillation process, but it was discovered that the wood casks imparted natural wood flavors to the wine, changing and improving the flavor. Thus, brandy was born. Here, this oak-y alcohol pairs with the sweet potato to create a Southern favorite—with a high-class twist.

Preheat the oven to 425°F.

Steam the sweet potatoes until they are fork-tender, about 10 minutes; remove from the steamer and mash or purée in a food processor until smooth. Set aside to cool.

In a large bowl, whisk together the brown sugar, cinnamon, salt, allspice, and nutmeg until well combined.

Add the brandy, eggs, sweet potato, and evaporated milk; whisk until smooth.

Pour the mixture into the pastry crust and place on a baking sheet.

Bake in the lower third of the oven for 15 minutes, then reduce the heat to 350°F and bake for an additional 40–45 minutes, or until the filling is set at the edges and just slightly wobbly in the center. Cool for 3 hours on a wire rack before slicing.

Maple Walnut Pie

SERVES 8

2 tablespoons all-purpose flour

½ cup packed light brown sugar

2 eggs

¾ cup corn syrup

⅓ cup maple syrup

¼ teaspoon salt

2 tablespoons butter, melted

1 teaspoon vanilla

1 cup chopped walnuts, toasted

1 (9") Mealy Pie Crust (see Chapter 1), unbaked

Maple syrup comes in various grades and colors—all of them delicious. But if you think that you should use the highest quality maple syrup for baking, you would be wrong. The highest quality maple syrups are best used as a topping, such as on pancakes and waffles. Grading systems vary by country, but a Grade B, or darker syrup, will provide a richer, rounder flavor on your not-so-humble pie.

Preheat the oven to 350°F.

Whisk together the flour and sugar.

Add the eggs, corn syrup, maple syrup, salt, butter, and vanilla and mix well.

Spread the walnuts into the crust in an even layer. Pour the filling over the walnuts and tap the pie gently on the counter to release any air bubbles.

Place the pie on a baking sheet and bake for 50–60 minutes, or until the filling is puffed all over and set. Cool to room temperature before serving.

White Chocolate Chiffon Pie

SERVES 8

1 tablespoon unflavored powdered gelatin

¼ cup cold water

4 egg yolks

1 cup sugar, divided

2 ounces white chocolate, melted

4 egg whites

¼ teaspoon salt

1 teaspoon vanilla

1 (9") Traditional Graham Cracker Crust (see Chapter 1), baked and cooled

1 recipe Stabilized Whipped Cream (see Chapter 2)

Don't let the ultralight texture of a chiffon pie fool you. The filling may look like a fluffy cloud, but it packs a lot of flavor. This pie is the place to use the highest quality white chocolate that you can find for the best flavor and smoothest texture. For some extra flavor, and a striking visual contrast, try using a chocolate cookie crust or topping each slice with fresh strawberries or cherries.

In a small bowl, combine the gelatin and the water. Allow to stand until completely bloomed, about 10 minutes.

In a double boiler, combine the egg yolks with ½ cup of the sugar. Whisk until thickened, about 10 minutes.

Remove from the heat and add the bloomed gelatin and melted chocolate. Whisk until completely dissolved. Allow to cool until the mixture begins to thicken.

In a large bowl, whip the egg whites with the salt until they are very frothy, about 30 seconds. Gradually add in the vanilla and remaining sugar, beating constantly, until the whites form medium peaks, about 1 minute.

Working in thirds, fold the egg whites into the white chocolate mixture, making sure no large streaks of egg white remain. Pour the mixture into the Traditional Graham Cracker Crust and chill until firm, about 4 hours.

Once chilled, prepare the Stabilized Whipped Cream and top the pie. Chill for 30 minutes before serving.

Orange and Dark Chocolate Cheese Pie

SERVES 8

2 cups orange juice

6 ounces cream cheese, softened

2 ounces bittersweet chocolate, melted and cooled

1 cup powdered sugar

1 cup heavy cream

2 tablespoons Dutch-processed cocoa powder

½ teaspoon vanilla

1 (9") Traditional Graham Cracker Crust (see Chapter 1), baked and cooled

2 tablespoons candied orange peel

Grated chocolate, for garnish

Candied orange peel adds a little crunchy texture and a pop of bright color to the top of this pie. If you can't fine candied orange peel, make your own. Combine fresh orange peel and water and bring to a boil for about 15 minutes. Rinse the peel well then simmer the orange peel in equal parts sugar and water for 45 minutes in a covered pot. Strain out the peels and roll them in sugar. Allow to dry completely. Try dipping these in dark chocolate for a delicious treat!

In a medium saucepan over medium heat, add the orange juice and bring to a simmer. Cook, stirring occasionally, until reduced to ¼ cup, about 20 minutes. Cool completely to room temperature.

In a large bowl, cream together the orange syrup, cream cheese, melted chocolate, and powdered sugar. Mix until smooth, then set aside.

In a separate bowl, whip the cream with the cocoa powder and vanilla until it forms medium peaks, about 1½ minutes.

Fold the cream into the orange mixture until no streaks of cream remain.

Pour the mixture into the Traditional Graham Cracker Crust and garnish with the candied orange peel and grated chocolate. Chill for 4 hours before serving.

Zucchini Pie

SERVES 8

4 medium zucchini, peeled, seeded, and sliced 1" thick

2 eggs

1½ cups sugar

¼ cup all-purpose flour

½ teaspoon salt

¼ cup butter

2 cups evaporated milk

1 teaspoon vanilla

½ teaspoon cinnamon

¼ teaspoon fresh-grated nutmeg

1 (9") Mealy Pie Crust (see Chapter 1), unbaked

Zucchini, which you can buy fresh at your local farmers' market, seems to find its way into all kinds of desserts from quick breads to brownies and cookies because it plays well with sugar, spices, and chocolate. Here, the zucchini is puréed and mixed with warm spices to create a delicious filling for this sophisticated pie.

Boil the zucchini until it is fork-tender, about 8–10 minutes. Drain well and allow to cool.

Preheat the oven to 375°F.

In a blender or food processor, blend the zucchini until smooth.

Pour the zucchini into a large bowl; add the eggs, sugar, flour, salt, and butter and whisk until smooth.

Add the milk, vanilla, cinnamon, and nutmeg; whisk until well combined.

Carefully pour the mixture into the pastry crust. Place the pie on a baking sheet and bake in the lower third of the oven for 20 minutes.

Reduce the heat to 350°F and cook for an additional 35–45 minutes, or until the pie is set and a thin knife inserted into the center of the pie comes out mostly clean. Cool completely before serving.

Cardamom and Saffron Chiffon Pie

SERVES 8

1 tablespoon unflavored powdered gelatin

¼ cup cold water

¼ teaspoon saffron threads

1 tablespoon warm water

4 egg yolks

⅓ cup sugar

3 cardamom pods, crushed

½ cup lime juice

4 egg whites

¼ teaspoon salt

¼ cup sugar

1 (9") All-Butter Pie Crust (see Chapter 1), baked and cooled

1 recipe Stabilized Whipped Cream (see Chapter 2)

Combined with the brightness of lime, spices cardamom and saffron shine in this light and airy pie. Cardamom has a floral, almost citrus flavor and can be purchased in pods or ground. If you cannot find cardamom pods, substitute ¼ teaspoon ground cardamom. Saffron has an earthy and slightly bitter flavor. It can be quite expensive, but remember that a little goes a long way.

In a small bowl, combine the gelatin and the water. Allow to stand until completely bloomed, about 10 minutes.

In another small bowl, combine the saffron and warm water. Allow to steep for 10 minutes.

In a double boiler, combine the egg yolks, sugar, cardamom pods, saffron with the water, and lime juice. Cook the mixture, whisking constantly, until thickened and lighter in color, about 10 minutes.

Remove from the heat and pour through a strainer into a large bowl. Add the bloomed gelatin and whisk until dissolved. Allow to cool until it starts to thicken, about 20 minutes.

In a large bowl, whip the egg whites with the salt until they are very frothy, about 30 seconds. Gradually add in the sugar, beating constantly, until the whites form medium peaks, about 1 minute.

Working in thirds, fold the egg whites into the saffron mixture, making sure no large streaks of egg white remain. Pour the mixture into the prepared crust and chill until firm, about 4 hours.

Once chilled, prepare the Stabilized Whipped Cream and top the pie. Chill for 30 minutes before serving.

Tiramisu Pie

SERVES 8

6 ounces cream cheese, softened

1 cup powdered sugar

3 tablespoons cold strongly brewed coffee, divided

½ teaspoon powdered gelatin

1 cup heavy cream

½ teaspoon vanilla

1 (9") Traditional Graham Cracker Crust (see Chapter 1), baked and cooled

1 recipe Stabilized Whipped Cream (see Chapter 2)

Cocoa powder, for dusting

If you thought tiramisu was exquisite, wait until you try it as a pie! The mascarpone cheese, often referred to as Italian cream cheese, brings an upscale, mild, and slightly tangy flavor and a texture that's soft, very smooth, and spreadable. Aside from its use in desserts, mascarpone can be spread on toasted bread or bagels, stirred into risotto, and served with fresh fruit for a simple dessert.

In a large bowl, cream together the cream cheese, powdered sugar, and 2 tablespoons of the coffee until thick and creamy.

In a small bowl, combine the remaining coffee with the gelatin. Allow to stand for 10 minutes to bloom. Once bloomed, heat in the microwave for 10 seconds to melt. Cool to room temperature.

In a medium bowl, beat the heavy cream with the vanilla until it begins to thicken, about 1 minute. Slowly add in the gelatin mixture and beat until medium peaks form, about 1 minute more.

Fold the whipped cream into the cream cheese mixture. Spread into the Traditional Graham Cracker Crust, then cover and chill for 4 hours.

Once chilled, prepare the Stabilized Whipped Cream and spread it over the pie. Chill for 1 hour. Dust the pie with cocoa powder before serving.

Vanilla Rum Meringue Pie

SERVES 8

1 (9") Cream Cheese Pastry Crust (see Chapter 1), unbaked

2 cups half-and-half

⅔ cup sugar

1 vanilla bean, split and the seeds scraped out

¼ cup cornstarch

2 eggs

¼ teaspoon salt

2 tablespoons butter

1 tablespoon spiced rum

1 recipe Foolproof Meringue (see Chapter 2)

Did you ever wonder what spices are used to make spiced rum? Every distiller has their own blend, but some of the spices used include cinnamon, vanilla, rosemary, allspice, clove, and pepper. The rum in this recipe infuses your pie with a grown-up flavor that is as at home on your kitchen table as it is at your friend's cocktail party.

Preheat the oven to 375°F. Line the pie crust with parchment paper or a double layer of aluminum foil and add pie weights or dry beans.

Bake for 15 minutes, then remove the paper and weights and bake for an additional 10–12 minutes, or until the crust is golden brown all over. Remove from the oven and set aside to cool.

In a medium saucepan, combine the half-and-half, sugar, vanilla bean and seeds, cornstarch, eggs, and salt and whisk until smooth. Cook over medium heat, stirring constantly, until it begins to boil and thicken, about 8 minutes.

Remove from the heat and add the butter and rum. Stir until the butter is melted. Pour through a strainer into a separate bowl, then pour directly into the prepared crust.

Place a layer of cling film directly on the custard and chill for 2 hours.

Preheat the oven to 450°F.

Prepare the Foolproof Meringue and spread over the pie. Bake for 6–8 minutes, or until golden brown. Cool completely to room temperature before serving.

Butternut Squash Pie

SERVES 8

1 medium butternut squash

1 cup packed light brown sugar

1 teaspoon ground cinnamon

½ teaspoon salt

¼ teaspoon fresh-grated nutmeg

2 eggs

12 ounces evaporated milk

½ teaspoon vanilla

1 (9") Mealy Pie Crust (see Chapter 1), unbaked

Traditionally reserved for holiday dinners, the butternut squash in this recipe makes this pie shine. Butternut squash has a naturally sweet flavor that is enhanced by roasting, which gives the squash a slight caramelized flavor and deep orange color. Roasting the squash will also help differentiate the flavor of this pie from its cousin, the traditional pumpkin pie.

Preheat the oven to 425°F.

Cut the top and bottom off the butternut squash, then cut the squash in half length-wise and scrape out the seeds.

Place the squash cut-side down on a parchment-lined baking sheet and roast for 45–55 minutes, or until a paring knife slips easily through the flesh.

Cool to room temperature. Scoop out the flesh and purée in a blender until smooth. It should yield approximately 1½ cups. Supplement with pumpkin purée, if needed.

In a large bowl, whisk together the sugar, cinnamon, salt, and nutmeg until well combined. Add the eggs, squash purée, evaporated milk, and vanilla. Whisk until smooth.

Pour the mixture into the prepared pastry crust and place on a sheet pan. Bake in the lower third of the oven for 15 minutes.

Reduce the heat to 350°F and bake for an additional 40–45 minutes, or until the filling is set at the edges and just slightly wobbly in the center. Cool for 3 hours on a wire rack before slicing.

Limoncello Mousse Pie

SERVES 8

1 (9") All-Butter Pie Crust (see Chapter 1), unbaked

1¼ cups milk

¼ cup limoncello

1 tablespoon lemon zest

½ cup sugar

3 tablespoons cornstarch

2 egg yolks

¼ teaspoon salt

1 tablespoon butter

1 teaspoon vanilla

½ teaspoon powdered gelatin

1 tablespoon cold water

1 cup heavy whipping cream

3 tablespoons powdered sugar

1 teaspoon vanilla

Limoncello, a lemon liqueur produced in the southern part of Italy, is traditionally served chilled after dinner to aid in digestion. It gives this dish a clean, sweet flavor with none of the tart, bitter flavor of fresh lemon juice. If you are not a fan of lemon, try orangecello in its place. It has a mild, sweet, aromatic orange flavor.

Preheat the oven to 375°F. Line the pie crust with parchment paper or a double layer of aluminum foil and add pie weights or dry beans.

Bake for 15 minutes, then remove the paper and weights and bake for an additional 10–12 minutes, or until the crust is golden brown all over. Remove from the oven and set aside to cool.

In a medium saucepan, combine the milk, limoncello, lemon zest, sugar, cornstarch, egg yolks, and salt and whisk until smooth. Cook over medium heat, stirring constantly, until it begins to simmer and thicken, about 8 minutes.

Remove from the heat and add the butter and vanilla; stir until melted. Pour through a strainer into a separate bowl. Place a layer of cling film directly on the custard and chill for 1 hour.

In a small bowl, mix the powdered gelatin with the cold water. Let stand 10 minutes, then melt in the microwave for 10 seconds. Allow to cool for 5 minutes, or until cool to the touch.

In a medium bowl, add the cream, powdered sugar, and vanilla. Whip on medium-high speed until it starts to thicken, about 1 minute.

Slowly pour in the cooled gelatin and whip until the cream forms medium peaks, about 1 minute. Cover and chill for 30 minutes.

Add ½ of the whipped cream to the limoncello mixture and gently fold to incorporate. Pour into the prepared crust and garnish the top with the remaining whipped cream. Chill for 4 hours before serving.

Pineapple Chiffon Pie

SERVES 8

1 tablespoon unflavored powdered gelatin

¼ cup cold water

4 egg yolks

⅓ cup sugar

1 cup crushed pineapple, drained

1 tablespoon lemon juice

4 egg whites

¼ teaspoon salt

¼ cup sugar

1 (9") Graham Pecan Crust (see Chapter 1), baked and cooled

1 recipe Stabilized Whipped Cream (see Chapter 2)

In this refreshing pie, sweet tart pineapple is whipped into a delicate chiffon filling. When making chiffon pies it is important to remember that they contain uncooked egg whites. The consumption of uncooked or undercooked eggs is not usually a problem for healthy adults. It can, however, cause problems for children, pregnant women, the elderly, or those with certain illnesses. When making any recipe that calls for uncooked or undercooked eggs, you can use pasteurized eggs. The pasteurization process kills the harmful bacteria, making them a better choice.

In a small bowl, combine the gelatin and the water. Allow to stand until completely bloomed, about 10 minutes.

In a double boiler, combine the egg yolks, sugar, pineapple, and lemon juice. Cook the mixture, whisking constantly, until thickened, about 10 minutes. Remove from the heat and add the bloomed gelatin. Whisk until dissolved. Allow to cool until it thickens.

In a large bowl, whip the egg whites with the salt until they are very frothy, about 30 seconds. Gradually add in the sugar, beating constantly, until the whites form medium peaks, about 1 minute.

Working in thirds, fold the egg whites into the pineapple mixture, making sure no large streaks of egg white remain. Pour the mixture into the prepared crust and chill until firm, about 4 hours.

Once chilled, prepare the Stabilized Whipped Cream and top the pie. Chill for 30 minutes before serving.

White Chocolate and Prosecco Mousse Pie

SERVES 8

1 (9") All-Butter Pie Crust (see Chapter 1), unbaked

½ cup sugar

2 egg yolks

½ cup prosecco

¼ teaspoon salt

1 ounce white chocolate, melted and cooled

1 teaspoon powdered gelatin

2 tablespoons cold water

1 cup heavy whipping cream

3 tablespoons powdered sugar

1 teaspoon vanilla

Shaved white chocolate, for garnish

Prosecco is Italian sparkling white wine. It is usually more affordable than French Champagne or California sparkling wine, and it has a lovely dry finish. In this pie, prosecco is used to brighten the flavor of the mousse and to give it a lighter texture. Unlike champagne, which gets a second long fermentation in the bottle, prosecco is fermented in glass tanks. This method is used for producing large quantities of wine with the fresh flavor preserved. When shopping buy prosecco within three years of its production date for the best flavor.

Preheat the oven to 375°F. Line the pie crust with parchment paper or a double layer of aluminum foil, and add pie weights or dry beans. Bake for 15 minutes, then remove the paper and weights and bake for an additional 10–12 minutes, or until the crust is golden brown all over. Remove from the oven and set aside to cool.

In a double boiler, combine the sugar and egg yolks until the egg yolks start to lighten in color; add the prosecco and salt. Whisk the mixture constantly until smooth, then cook, beating constantly, until it begins to lighten in color and thicken, about 8 minutes.

Beat in the melted white chocolate until well combined and smooth. Carefully remove the bowl from the heat and place directly into an ice bath. Cool, stirring occasionally, until the mixture reaches room temperature.

In a small bowl, mix the powdered gelatin with the cold water. Let stand 10 minutes, then melt in the microwave for 10 seconds. Allow to cool for 10 minutes, or until cool to the touch. Stir half of the gelatin mixture into the prosecco mixture.

In a medium bowl, add the cream, powdered sugar, and vanilla. Using a hand mixer, whip on medium-high speed until it starts to thicken, about 1 minute.

Slowly pour in the remaining cooled gelatin and whip until the cream forms medium peaks, about 1 minute more.

Add ½ of the whipped cream to the chocolate mixture and gently fold to incorporate. Pour into the prepared crust and chill for 4 hours before serving. Garnish with the remaining whipped cream and shaved chocolate.

White Chocolate Lime Mascarpone Cheese Pie

SERVES 8

¼ cup lime juice

1 teaspoon lime zest

6 ounces mascarpone cheese, softened

2 ounces white chocolate, melted and cooled

1 cup powdered sugar

½ teaspoon powdered gelatin

1 tablespoon cold water

1 cup heavy cream

½ teaspoon vanilla

1 (9") Traditional Graham Cracker Crust (see Chapter 1), baked and cooled

Fresh lime and white chocolate make for a beautiful—if surprising—pairing. The tart but not acerbic citrus helps cut the buttery richness of the white chocolate. This recipe uses mascarpone cheese to give this pie its creamy smooth texture, but you can use cream cheese if you prefer. If you are serving this pie for guests, garnish the top with fresh lime zest and finely grated white chocolate just before serving.

In a large bowl, cream together the lime juice, lime zest, mascarpone cheese, melted white chocolate, and powdered sugar. Mix until smooth, then set aside.

In a small bowl, mix the powdered gelatin with the cold water. Let stand 10 minutes, then melt in the microwave for 10 seconds. Allow to cool for 5 minutes, or until cool to the touch.

In a medium bowl, add the cream and vanilla. Using a hand mixer, whip on medium-high speed until it starts to thicken, about 1 minute.

Slowly pour in the cooled gelatin and whip until the cream forms medium peaks, about 1 minute.

Fold the cream into the white chocolate mixture until no streaks of cream remain.

Pour the mixture into the prepared crust and chill for 4 hours before serving.

Key Lime Coconut Pie

SERVES 8

5 egg yolks

1 cup unsweetened coconut milk

14 ounces sweetened condensed milk

½ cup key lime juice

1 (9") Traditional Graham Cracker Crust (see Chapter 1), baked and cooled

1 recipe Stabilized Whipped Cream (see Chapter 2)

¼ cup shredded sweetened coconut, toasted

This pie takes a tropical twist on the everyday key lime pie by adding coconut milk and toasted coconut. Do not confuse coconut milk with coconut cream or cream of coconut. Coconut milk is simply the liquid that is pressed out of the coconut flesh. Coconut cream or cream of coconut is a coconut-flavored sugar syrup that is used for making cocktails.

Preheat the oven to 350°F.

Lightly whisk the egg yolks until they are broken.

Add the unsweetened coconut milk and sweetened condensed milk and stir to combine.

Add the lime juice and stir until smooth.

Pour the filling into the prepared crust. Bake for 25–30 minutes, or until set around the edges but still slightly wobbly in the center. Cool on a wire rack for 1 hour, then chill in the refrigerator for at least 4 hours, or overnight. When ready to serve, prepare the Stabilized Whipped Cream and spread it evenly over the pie. Garnish with the toasted coconut. Chill for 30 minutes before serving.

Strawberry Chiffon Pie

SERVES 8

1 tablespoon unflavored powdered gelatin

¼ cup cold water

1 cup crushed strawberries

1 cup sugar

½ cup hot water

¼ teaspoon salt

1 tablespoon lemon juice

2 egg whites

2 tablespoons sugar

1 (9") Traditional Graham Cracker Crust (see Chapter 1), baked and cooled

1 recipe Stabilized Whipped Cream (see Chapter 2)

Strawberries are not really berries. In fact, they are a seed-bearing fruit. But no matter what they are, they are decadent both when eaten just as they are or when made into a beautiful dessert. One common problem of strawberry desserts is that once cooked, they can lose some of their robust red color. If that color is important to you, a drop of red food coloring will perk things right up.

In a small bowl, combine the gelatin and the water. Allow to stand until completely bloomed, about 10 minutes.

Combine the crushed strawberries and sugar and allow to stand for 10 minutes.

Mix the bloomed gelatin with the hot water until dissolved, then whisk it into the strawberries along with the salt and lemon juice. Let the mixture stand until it begins to thicken, about 10 minutes.

In a large bowl, whip the egg whites until they are very frothy, about 30 seconds. Gradually add in the sugar, beating constantly, until the whites form medium peaks, about 1 minute.

Working in thirds, fold the egg whites into the strawberry mixture, making sure no large streaks of egg white remain.

Pour the mixture into the prepared crust and chill until firm, about 4 hours.

Once chilled, prepare the Stabilized Whipped Cream and top the pie. Chill for 30 minutes before serving.

Chocolate Almond Pie

SERVES 8

2 ounces unsweetened chocolate, chopped

2 tablespoons butter

2 eggs

2 egg yolks

½ cup light brown sugar

⅓ cup corn syrup

⅓ cup almond butter

1 teaspoon vanilla

1 tablespoon cocoa powder

¾ cup toasted almonds, chopped

1 (9") Almond Pastry Crust (see Chapter 1), unbaked

Almond butter can be found in most grocery stores; however, you can also make it yourself at home in a food processor. Roughly chop the almonds before processing to save wear and tear on your food processor's blade. If you toast the almonds slightly before puréeing, you'll enhance their natural nutty flavor.

Preheat the oven to 375°F.

In a double boiler, melt the chocolate and butter. Remove from the heat.

In a large bowl, combine the eggs, egg yolks, sugar, corn syrup, and almond butter. Add in the melted chocolate, vanilla, and cocoa powder.

Spread the almonds into the bottom of the pastry crust then pour the mixture over the top. Place on a baking sheet and cook for 40–50 minutes, or until the filling is just set. Serve slightly warm.

Parsnip Custard Pie

SERVES 8

2 pounds fresh parsnips, trimmed and peeled

1 cup packed light brown sugar

1 teaspoon ground cinnamon

½ teaspoon salt

¼ teaspoon ground ginger

¼ teaspoon fresh-grated nutmeg

2 eggs

12 ounces evaporated milk

1 teaspoon vanilla

1 (9") Lard Crust (see Chapter 1), unbaked

Perhaps unexpected in a pie, the parsnip is a root vegetable that is related to the carrot; in fact, the parsnip looks a lot like a carrot except it has a pale white color, and is full of the same vitamins and minerals, particularly potassium. Parsnips are sweet and almost buttery once cooked, and once they are puréed they have a texture similar to that of pumpkin purée.

Preheat the oven to 425°F.

Bring a large pot of water to a boil. Add the parsnips and cook until fork tender, about 12–15 minutes. Drain the parsnips and then transfer to a blender or food processor and blend until smooth. It should yield approximately 1½ cups. Supplement with pumpkin purée, if needed.

In a large bowl, whisk together the sugar, cinnamon, salt, ginger, and nutmeg until well combined.

Add the eggs, squash purée, evaporated milk, and vanilla. Whisk until smooth.

Pour the mixture into the prepared pastry crust and place on a sheet pan. Bake in the lower third of the oven for 15 minutes.

Reduce the heat to 350°F and bake for an additional 40–45 minutes, or until the filling is set at the edges and just slightly wobbly in the center. Cool for 3 hours on a wire rack before slicing.

Black-Bottom Tiramisu Pie

SERVES 8

2 tablespoons heavy cream

¼ teaspoon instant espresso powder

2 ounces bittersweet chocolate (at least 65 percent), chopped

1 (9") Traditional Graham Cracker Crust (see Chapter 1), baked and cooled

6 ounces cream cheese, softened

1 cup powdered sugar

3 tablespoons cold strongly brewed coffee, divided

½ teaspoon powdered gelatin

1 cup heavy cream

½ teaspoon vanilla

Cocoa powder, for dusting

A thin layer of bittersweet chocolate espresso ganache is hidden, like a little treasure, in the bottom of this pie. Espresso powder is a fantastic way to amp up the flavor of chocolate, and in this pie it is found in both the filling and the ganache, where it serves to tie them together.

In a small bowl, heat the heavy cream and espresso powder in the microwave until very hot and steamy, about 1 minute.

Add in the chopped chocolate and allow to stand for 1 minute, then whisk until very smooth. Carefully pour into the Traditional Graham Cracker Crust and spread to form an even layer. Chill for 1 hour in the refrigerator.

In a large bowl, cream together the cream cheese, powdered sugar, and 2 tablespoons of the coffee until thick and creamy.

In a small bowl, combine the remaining coffee with the gelatin. Allow to stand for 10 minutes to bloom. Once bloomed, heat in the microwave for 10 seconds to melt. Cool to room temperature.

In a medium bowl, beat the heavy cream with the vanilla until it begins to thicken, about 1 minute.

Slowly add in the gelatin mixture and beat until medium peaks form, about 1 minute.

Fold the whipped cream into the cream cheese mixture. Spread into the pie crust over the chocolate layer, cover, and chill for 4 hours.

Once chilled, prepare the Stabilized Whipped Cream and spread it over the pie. Chill for 1 hour. Dust the pie with cocoa powder before serving.

Triple-Layer Mousse Pie

SERVES 8

1 (9") All-Butter Pie Crust
(see Chapter 1), unbaked

1½ cups milk

½ cup sugar

2 tablespoons cornstarch

2 egg yolks

¼ teaspoon salt

1 tablespoon butter

1 teaspoon vanilla

1 ounce bittersweet chocolate, chopped

1 teaspoon powdered gelatin

2 tablespoons cold water

2 cups heavy whipping
cream

¼ cup powdered sugar

1 teaspoon vanilla

Shaved chocolate, for
garnish

Some pies are beautiful in the pie dish, but the sophistication doesn't carry over to the plate. But this pie is as pretty sliced as it is whole. If you want to add an extra dimension to this not-so-humble pie, try serving it in a pretzel or chocolate cookie crust. Not only will they provide an extra kick in the flavor department, they will also add to the pie's already striking visual appeal.

Preheat the oven to 375°F. Line the pie crust with parchment paper or a double layer of aluminum foil and add pie weights or dry beans. Bake for 15 minutes, then remove the paper and weights. Bake for an additional 10–12 minutes, or until the crust is golden brown all over. Remove from the oven and set aside to cool.

In a medium saucepan, combine the milk, sugar, cornstarch, egg yolks, and salt. Whisk until smooth, then cook over medium heat, stirring constantly, until it begins to boil and thicken, about 10 minutes. Remove from the heat and add the butter and vanilla; stir until melted. Pour through a strainer then divide into 2 bowls.

Stir the chopped chocolate into 1 bowl until melted and smooth. Place a layer of cling film directly on the custards and chill for 1 hour.

In a small bowl, mix the powdered gelatin with the cold water. Let stand 10 minutes, then melt in the microwave for 10 seconds. Allow to cool for 10 minutes, or until cool to the touch.

In a medium bowl, add the cream, powdered sugar, and vanilla. Using a hand mixer, whip at medium-high speed until it starts to thicken, about 1 minute. Slowly pour in the cooled gelatin and whip until the cream forms medium peaks, about 1 minute. Cover and chill for 30 minutes.

Add ¼ of the whipped cream to the chocolate mixture and gently fold to incorporate. Add ⅓ of the remaining whipped cream to the vanilla mixture and gently fold to incorporate.

Spread the chocolate mixture into the prepared crust, then carefully spread over the vanilla mixture. Cover and chill for 4 hours before serving. Garnish with the remaining whipped cream and shaved chocolate.

Sweet Potato Meringue Pie

SERVES 8

3 medium sweet potatoes, baked until fork-tender

¾ cup sugar

1 teaspoon cinnamon

¼ teaspoon salt

¼ teaspoon allspice

¼ teaspoon ground cloves

⅛ teaspoon fresh-grated nutmeg

2 eggs

12 ounces evaporated milk

1 (9") Mealy Pie Crust (see Chapter 1), unbaked

1 recipe Foolproof Meringue (see Chapter 2)

Did you know that a sweet potato is cured as soon as it's harvested? The curing process takes between ten days to three weeks, and during that time the natural starches in the tuber convert to sugar, which then sweetens this light, delicious pie! Never store sweet potatoes in the refrigerator because their flavor will change when chilled. Instead, keep them in a cool, dark place with good ventilation for longest shelf life.

Preheat the oven to 425°F.

Peel the sweet potatoes and add the flesh to a large bowl. Add the sugar, cinnamon, salt, allspice, cloves, and nutmeg; whisk until well combined.

Add the eggs and evaporated milk and whisk until smooth.

Pour the mixture into the pastry crust and place on a baking sheet. Bake in the lower third of the oven for 10 minutes.

Reduce the heat to 350°F and bake for an additional 40–45 minutes, or until the filling is set at the edges and just slightly wobbly in the center. Remove the pie and turn up the oven to 450°F.

Prepare the Foolproof Meringue and spread over the top of the hot pie. Return to the oven for 10–12 minutes, or until the meringue is golden brown. Cool to room temperature before serving.

∽ Chapter 4 ∾

Fruits, Nuts, and Berries

Classic flavors are classic for a reason—and pies made with fruit, nuts, and berries are among the most popular of the traditional flavors. They're also among the most memorable pies. Maybe your memory is of sticky and sweet pecan pie or of a slice of warm apple pie topped with a scoop of slowly melting vanilla ice cream? That's great, but it's time to take these pies from grandma to grown-up! The recipes in this chapter showcase intriguing ingredients like lavender, tea, cheese, and roasted chilies that you can use to spice up these old favorites, but it doesn't stop there! You'll also find exciting flavor profiles borrowed from French pastries, exotic spices, and buttery cookies that you'll incorporate into these modern masterpieces. So say goodbye to your grandmother's apple pie and get cooking!

Bourbon Pecan Pie

SERVES 8

8 ounces cream cheese, softened

1 tablespoon bourbon

1 cup powdered sugar, divided

1 cup heavy cream

1 teaspoon vanilla

1½ cups chopped pecans, toasted, plus more for garnish

1 (9") Graham Pecan Crust (see Chapter 1), baked and cooled

1 batch Salted Caramel Sauce (see Chapter 2)

All bourbon is whiskey, but not all whiskey is bourbon. In the United States as well as other countries, whiskey must meet certain manufacturing requirements to legally carry the name *bourbon*. Bourbon is aged in charred oak barrels, which imparts the distinctive, complex flavors and caramel color that you'll find in this pie.

In a large bowl, cream together the cream cheese, bourbon, and ½ cup of the powdered sugar. Set aside.

In a separate bowl, whip the heavy cream with the remaining powdered sugar and vanilla until it forms medium peaks, about 1 minute.

Beat the whipped cream into the cream cheese mixture until almost combined. Add the chopped pecans and fold until evenly mixed.

Pour into the prepared crust and chill overnight. Serve with a drizzle of Salted Caramel Sauce.

Apple Pie with a Spicy Cheddar Crust

SERVES 8

3 medium Granny Smith apples, peeled, cored, and sliced ¼" thick

3 medium Golden Delicious apples, peeled, cored, and sliced ¼" thick

2 tablespoons lemon juice

½ cup packed light brown sugar

¼ cup all-purpose flour

¼ teaspoon salt

1 teaspoon cinnamon

¼ teaspoon fresh-grated nutmeg

½ teaspoon vanilla

1 (9" Spicy Cheddar Crust (see Chapter 1), unbaked)

1 egg, beaten

A little sweet, a little tangy, and just a little spicy, this pie pays homage to the classic combination of apple pie with a slice of cheese on top. This upscale version of this diner classic adds a hint of cayenne pepper that gives just a whisper of heat following the tangy sweetness of the apple filling.

Preheat the oven to 400°F.

Put the apple slices in a large bowl and toss with the lemon juice.

Add the brown sugar, flour, salt, cinnamon, nutmeg, and vanilla; toss to coat and set aside for 10 minutes.

Fill the pie crust with the apple mixture. Brush the edge of the bottom pie crust with the beaten egg so that the top crust will adhere. Top with the second crust and trim the dough to within 1" of the pan's edge. Tuck the edge of the top crust under the edge of the bottom crust. Crimp the dough using your fingers or a fork. Brush the entire top crust with the beaten egg and cut 4 or 5 slits in the top to vent steam.

Place the pie on a baking sheet and bake, in the lower third of the oven, for 1 hour to 1 hour and 15 minutes, or until the filling is bubbling in the center of the pie and the crust is golden brown all over. Enjoy warm.

Blood Orange Curd Pie

SERVES 8

1 cup sugar

1 tablespoon lime juice

1 cup blood orange juice

8 egg yolks

2 tablespoons cornstarch

8 tablespoons unsalted butter

1 (9") Traditional Graham Cracker Crust (see Chapter 1), baked and cooled

1 recipe Foolproof Meringue (see Chapter 2)

Blood oranges have a distinctive red-colored flesh and a sweet-tart flavor that carries over into this not-so-humble pie. Common to the Mediterranean, the blood orange is a popular ingredient in Italian cooking. This delicious fruit is also grown in Texas and California, where the days are warm but the evenings are cool. Look for blood oranges to hit your local produce market in the winter and early spring.

Preheat the oven to 375°F.

In a medium saucepan, combine the sugar, lime juice, and blood orange juice; stir until the sugar is melted.

Whisk in the egg yolks and cornstarch. Cook over medium heat, whisking constantly, until bubbling and thick, about 10 minutes.

Reduce the heat to low and stir in the butter until melted. Pour the curd through a strainer into the prepared crust.

Spread the Foolproof Meringue onto the filling while it is still hot, making sure the meringue completely covers the filling and the inside edge of the crust.

Bake for 10–12 minutes, or until the meringue is golden brown. Remove from the oven and chill for 3 hours, uncovered, before slicing.

Brandied Pear Pie

SERVES 8

1 (9") All-Butter Pie Crust
(see Chapter 1), unbaked

2 tablespoons unsalted
butter

8 medium Bosc pears,
peeled, cored, and sliced ¼"
thick

1 vanilla bean, split and
seeds scraped out

½ cup brandy, divided

½ cup sugar

¼ cup cornstarch

½ teaspoon cinnamon

¼ teaspoon salt

1 recipe Spiked Whipped
Cream (see Chapter 2),
made with brandy

When shopping for the pears used in this recipe, keep a few things in mind. Pears are harvested before they are ripe, and they ripen fairly quickly at room temperature, which means that it is best to buy fruit that is only slightly ripe at the store. You also want to avoid bruised or blemished skins, which indicate the fruit has been damaged or is past its prime. When the flesh at the stem end of the pear gives slightly under soft pressure it is ripe and ready to go into your pie.

Preheat the oven to 375°F.

Line the pie crust with parchment paper or a double layer of aluminum foil and add pie weights or dry beans. Bake for 10 minutes, then remove the paper and weights and bake for an additional 8–10 minutes, or until the crust is lightly golden brown all over. Remove from the oven and set aside to cool.

In a large skillet over medium heat, melt the butter until it foams. Add the sliced pears, vanilla bean, and vanilla bean seeds.

Remove the pan from the heat and add ¼ cup of the brandy and the sugar. Return the pan to the heat and cool until the pears are just starting to soften, about 3 minutes.

In a small bowl, whisk together the remaining brandy and the cornstarch until smooth. Add to the simmering fruit and stir until thickened, about 1 minute.

Remove from the heat and add the cinnamon and salt. Carefully remove the vanilla bean.

Fill the pie crust with the pear mixture. Place the pie on a baking sheet and bake, in the lower third of the oven, for 25–30 minutes, or until the filling is bubbling in the center of the pie and the crust is golden brown all over.

Cool the pie completely to room temperature, then top with the Spiked Whipped Cream. Serve immediately.

Vanilla Pear Pie

SERVES 8

1 cup sugar

⅓ cup cornstarch

¼ teaspoon cinnamon

Seeds of 1 vanilla bean pod or 2 teaspoons vanilla bean paste

8 Bosc pears, peeled, cored, and sliced ¼" thick

2 tablespoons brandy

1 (9") Mealy Pie Crust (see Chapter 1), unbaked

1 egg, beaten

1 (9") Flaky Pie Crust (see Chapter 1)

The vanilla beans found in this Vanilla Pear Pie are native to Mexico and South America. Vanilla is picked when it is still green and undergoes a fermentation process to develop the best flavor. When buying vanilla beans, look for plump, black beans that are shiny on the outside and not dry or stiff. Store vanilla beans in an airtight container for up to six months to preserve freshness.

Preheat the oven to 425°F.

In a large bowl, mix the sugar, cornstarch, and cinnamon until well blended.

Add vanilla bean, pears, and brandy; toss to coat. Allow to stand 10 minutes.

Fill the Mealy Pie Crust with the pear mixture. Brush the edge with the beaten egg so that the top crust will adhere. Top with the Flaky Pie Crust and trim the dough to within 1" of the pan's edge. Tuck the edge of the top crust under the edge of the bottom crust. Crimp the dough using your fingers or a fork. Brush the entire top crust with the beaten egg and cut 4 or 5 slits in the top to vent steam.

Place the pie on a baking sheet and bake for 20 minutes.

Reduce the heat to 350°F and bake for an additional 40–50 minutes, or until the pie is bubbling and the juices are thick. Cool for 2 hours before slicing.

Orange Honey Pecan Pie

SERVES 8

2 tablespoons all-purpose flour

½ cup packed light brown sugar

2 eggs

¾ cup honey

¼ teaspoon salt

2 tablespoons butter, melted

1 teaspoon vanilla

1 tablespoon orange zest

1½ cups coarsely chopped pecans

1 (9") Mealy Pie Crust (see Chapter 1), unbaked

The lush honey used in this recipe is classified by the flowers the bees used as a source for the nectar. Wildflower honey, for example, is honey that is made from multiple flower sources, such as clover, lavender, and wildflowers. Honey has complex flavors and, depending on the flowers used, it can range from mild and buttery to sharp and slightly citrus. Look for local honey or honey that is produced in small batches rather than honey that is mass produced; small batch honey will have a more intense floral flavor.

Preheat the oven to 350°F.

Whisk together the flour and light brown sugar. Add the eggs, honey, salt, butter, vanilla, and orange zest; whisk until smooth.

Spread the pecans into the crust in an even layer. Pour the filling over the pecans and tap the pie gently on the counter to release any air bubbles.

Place the pie on a baking sheet and bake for 50–60 minutes, or until the filling is puffed all over and set. Cool to room temperature before serving.

Lavender-Infused Lemon Curd Pie

SERVES 8

1 (10") Short Crust for Tarts (see Chapter 1), unbaked

¾ cup sugar

¾ cup lemon juice

1 teaspoon lemon zest

1 teaspoon dried lavender, lightly crushed

6 egg yolks

1 tablespoon cornstarch

6 tablespoons unsalted butter

½ recipe Stabilized Whipped Cream (see Chapter 2)

Culinary lavender has a pungent floral aroma that pairs exceptionally well with the lemon in this upscale recipe. Lavender can be found in most natural food stores, gourmet shops, and even at your local farmers' market. For extra lavender flavor, grind ¼ teaspoon with ¼ cup of sugar and sprinkle it over the top of each slice of pie as a fragrant and sophisticated garnish.

Preheat the oven to 350°F. Line the tart with parchment paper, or a double layer of aluminum foil, and add pie weights or dry beans.

Bake for 10 minutes, then remove the paper and weights and bake for an additional 10–12 minutes, or until the crust is golden brown all over. Remove from the oven and set aside to cool.

In a medium saucepan, combine the sugar and lemon juice and stir until the sugar is melted.

Whisk in the lemon zest, lavender, egg yolks, and cornstarch. Cook over medium heat, whisking constantly, until bubbling thick.

Reduce the heat to low and stir in the butter until melted. Pour the curd through a strainer into the prepared crust. Chill for 4 hours.

Once the tart has chilled, prepare the Stabilized Whipped Cream. Pipe the whipped cream around the edge of the tart. Chill for 30 minutes before serving.

Peach Ginger Hand Pies

SERVES 8

2 peaches, peeled, stoned, and finely diced

¼ cup packed light brown sugar

1 teaspoon fresh-grated ginger

¼ teaspoon cinnamon

1 tablespoon cornstarch

2 recipes Flaky Pie Crust (see Chapter 1), not pressed into pie pans

1 egg, beaten

Fresh ginger has a spicy heat that dry or powdered ginger sometimes lacks, so if you really want to up the ante on this not-so-humble pie, be sure to buy fresh. Fresh ginger should be firm to the touch, with no major blemishes to the skin. To peel ginger, you can use the bowl of a teaspoon to scrape away the skin. It comes off easily, since it is so thin. Store fresh ginger in the refrigerator for up to a week, or peel, mince, and freeze for up to a month.

In a medium saucepan over medium heat, combine the peaches, sugar, ginger, cinnamon, and cornstarch. Cook until the mixture comes to a boil and thickens, about 5 minutes. Remove from the heat and cool to room temperature.

Preheat the oven to 425°F. Line a baking sheet with parchment paper.

Cut the pastry into 8" rounds or squares. Place about ¼ cup filling into the pastry slightly off center. Brush the edges of the pastry with beaten egg and fold the dough over the filling. Pinch or crimp with a fork to seal.

Place the pies on the prepared baking sheet and brush with beaten egg. With scissors or a sharp paring knife, cut vents in pastry to vent steam.

Bake for 15 minutes, then reduce heat to 350°F and bake for an additional 25 minutes, or until the pastry is golden brown and juices are bubbling. Cool to room temperature before serving.

Honey Lavender Apple Pie

SERVES 8

¾ cup sugar

¼ cup honey

¼ cup cornstarch

½ teaspoon cinnamon

½ teaspoon fresh-grated nutmeg

½ teaspoon lavender, crushed

8 medium Gala or Honey-crisp apples, peeled, cored, and sliced ¼" thick

1 (9") Mealy Pie Crust (see Chapter 1), unbaked

1 egg, beaten

1 recipe Flaky Pie Crust (see Chapter 1), unbaked

Lavender lends an unexpected floral twist to what might be an otherwise ordinary apple pie. Not only is the pie flavored with lavender, it is also sweetened in part by honey, which adds its own aroma to the pie. If you like, you may add a teaspoon of fresh grated orange or lemon zest to this pie for a little citrus buzz.

Preheat the oven to 400°F.

In a large bowl, mix the sugar, honey, cornstarch, cinnamon, nutmeg, and lavender until well blended. Add the apples and toss to coat. Allow to stand 10 minutes.

Fill the Mealy Pie Crust with the apple mixture. Brush the edge of the crust with the beaten egg so the top crust will adhere. Top with the Flaky Pie Crust and trim the dough to within 1" of the pan's edge. Tuck the edge of the top crust under the edge of the bottom crust. Crimp the dough using your fingers or a fork. Brush the entire top crust with the beaten egg, and cut 4 or 5 slits in the top to vent steam.

Place the pie on a baking sheet and bake for 20 minutes.

Reduce the heat to 350°F and bake for an additional 33–40 minutes, or until the pie is bubbling and the juices are thick. Cool for 2 hours before slicing.

Roasted Hatch Chilies, Apple, and Ricotta Hand Pies

SERVES 8

1 tablespoon butter

½ onion, finely diced

1 Granny Smith Apple, peeled, cored, and finely diced

1 cup ricotta cheese

½ cup shredded sharp Cheddar cheese

2 eggs

½ teaspoon salt

3 fire-roasted mild Hatch or other mild chili peppers, seeded and sliced into thin strips

2 recipes Flaky Pie Crust (see Chapter 1), not pressed into pie pans

Hatch chilies are cultivated in Hatch, New Mexico, and arrive in markets in the Southwest around August. They range from mild and sweet to as spicy as the jalapeño. If you live outside of an area where hatch chilies can be purchased fresh, they are also available frozen and canned.

In a medium skillet over medium heat, add the butter. Once it begins to foam, add the onion and cook, stirring often, until softened, about 3 minutes.

Add the apples and cook until they just begin to soften, about 2 minutes. Remove the pan from the heat and allow the mixture to cool to room temperature.

In a large bowl, combine the ricotta cheese, Cheddar cheese, 1 egg, and salt. Mix until smooth, then add the diced chilies and onion mixture. Mix until evenly combined.

Preheat the oven to 425°F. Line a baking sheet with parchment paper.

Cut the pastry into 8" rounds or squares. Divide the filling evenly between the pastry circles, making sure to place the filling slightly off center.

Brush the edges of the pastry with beaten egg and fold the dough over the filling. Pinch or crimp with a fork to seal. Place the pies on the prepared baking sheet.

Beat the remaining egg and brush over the pies. With scissors or a sharp paring knife, cut vents in pastry to vent steam.

Bake for 10 minutes, then reduce heat to 350°F and bake for an additional 25–30 minutes, or until the pastry is golden brown and the filling is steamy. Remove from the oven and allow to cool for 10 minutes before serving.

Tea-Infused Pear Pie

SERVES 8

1 (9") All-Butter Pie Crust (see Chapter 1), unbaked

¼ cup heavy cream

2 teaspoons black tea leaves or 1 tea bag

¼ cup cornstarch

2 tablespoons unsalted butter

8 medium Bosc pears, peeled, cored, and sliced ¼" thick

1 vanilla bean, split and seeds scraped out

½ cup sugar

½ teaspoon cinnamon

¼ teaspoon salt

1 recipe Spiked Whipped Cream (see Chapter 2), made with brandy

Black tea brings to this sophisticated pie a deep, aromatic flavor that is as complex as wine. This is the place to use the best quality tea available, since the flavor perfumes every bite of this scrumptious dessert. If you're looking for a lighter flavor, you can substitute jasmine tea, which has a very distinct floral taste, for the black tea in this recipe.

Preheat the oven to 375°F. Line the pie crust with parchment paper, or a double layer of aluminum foil, and add pie weights or dry beans.

Bake for 10 minutes, then remove the paper and weights and bake for an additional 8–10 minutes, or until the crust is lightly golden brown all over. Remove from the oven and set aside to cool.

In a small pot, heat the cream until it simmers. Add the tea leaves and stir to combine. Remove the pot from the heat, cover, and allow to steep for 10 minutes.

Strain the cream into a large bowl; whisk in the cornstarch. Set aside.

In a large skillet over medium heat, melt the butter until it foams. Add the sliced pears, vanilla bean, vanilla bean seeds, and sugar. Cook until the pears are just starting to soften, about 3 minutes.

Remove from the heat and add the cinnamon and salt. Carefully remove the vanilla bean and stir in the cream mixture.

Fill the pie crust with the pear mixture. Place the pie on a sheet pan and bake in the lower third of the oven for 25–30 minutes, or until the filling is bubbling in the center of the pie and the crust is golden brown all over.

Cool the pie completely to room temperature, then top with the Spiked Whipped Cream. Serve immediately.

Toffee Almond Pie

SERVES 8

1 stick unsalted butter, melted

½ cup packed light brown sugar

¾ cup light corn syrup

¼ teaspoon almond extract

1 teaspoon vanilla

3 eggs

1 cup sliced almonds, lightly toasted

½ cup toffee bits

1 (9") Cream Cheese Pastry Crust (see Chapter 1), unbaked

Almond-studded toffee is a candy shop favorite, and those flavors are used to make a grown-up version of this childhood treat. If you are unable to find toffee bits at the store, simply buy a toffee candy bar and crush it up with a rolling pin in a plastic bag. Those candy bars usually have a chocolate coating, which will add another layer of flavor to this pie.

Preheat the oven to 350°F.

In a large bowl, whisk together the butter, brown sugar, corn syrup, almond extract, vanilla, and eggs until well combined.

Spread the sliced almonds and toffee bits evenly in the bottom of the pastry crust, then pour the egg mixture over the top. Tap the pie gently on the counter to release any air bubbles.

Place the pie on a baking sheet and bake for 50–60 minutes, or until the filling is puffed all over and set. Cool to room temperature before serving.

Peach Sour Cream Pie

SERVES 8

1 (9") All-Butter Pie Crust (see Chapter 1), unbaked

1 cup sour cream

½ cup sugar

2 tablespoons cornstarch

2 eggs, lightly beaten

1 teaspoon vanilla

¼ teaspoon mace

8 medium peaches, peeled and cut into ¼" thick slices

1 recipe Butter Crumble (see Chapter 2)

In this palate-pleasing pie, sweet slices of peach are surrounded by tangy sour cream custard and topped with a crisp, buttery crumble. Mace, the lacy outer coating of the nutmeg, lends its slightly peppery citrus flavor to the sour cream filling. This pie is best served at room temperature or slightly chilled.

Preheat the oven to 425°F.

Line the pie crust with foil or parchment paper and fill with pie weights or dry beans. Bake for 10 minutes, then remove the lining and weights and bake for an additional 10 minutes. Set aside to cool.

In a large bowl, whisk together the sour cream, sugar, and cornstarch until smooth.

Add the eggs, vanilla, and mace and whisk until well combined. Fold in the sliced peaches.

Pour into the crust and top with the Butter Crumble. Bake for 30–35 minutes. Cool to room temperature before serving.

Apricot and Walnut Pie

SERVES 8

½ cup dried apricots, finely diced

1 cup orange juice

1 cup corn syrup

2 tablespoons unsalted butter, melted

½ cup sugar

¼ teaspoon cinnamon

1 tablespoon all-purpose flour

3 eggs

¼ teaspoon salt

¾ cup chopped walnuts

1 (9") Mealy Pie Crust (see Chapter 1), unbaked

Dry apricots have a sweet, mild flavor that is more concentrated than the fresh fruit; they add this concentrated flavor to anything to which they are added. When baking with dry fruits, it is a good idea to reconstitute them in a little juice prior to baking; giving them a good soak will add moisture and make them tender. Do not discard the juice used to soak the fruit. Instead, reduce it down into a sauce that can be drizzled over ice cream—or over cut slices of pie.

Preheat the oven to 350°F.

In a small saucepan, combine the diced apricots and orange juice. Bring the mixture to a boil, then remove the pot from the heat and allow to steep for 5 minutes. Strain the apricots and cool to room temperature.

In a large bowl, whisk together the corn syrup, butter, and sugar. Once well combined, add the cinnamon, flour, eggs, and salt. Whisk until smooth.

Spread the walnuts and apricots into the bottom of the pastry crust. Carefully pour the filling over the top.

Place on a baking sheet and bake for 45–55 minutes, or until the filling is puffed all over and set. Cool to room temperature before slicing.

Pineapple Macadamia Nut Pie

SERVES 8

1 stick unsalted butter, melted

¾ cup dark brown sugar

½ cup dark corn syrup

2 tablespoons dark rum

1 teaspoon vanilla

3 egg

⅓ cup crushed pineapple

1 cup chopped macadamia nuts, lightly toasted

1 (9") Mealy Pie Crust (see Chapter 1), unbaked

This fabulous pie is piled high with a deep, caramel-flavored custard with just a hint of molasses due to the dark corn syrup, dark brown sugar, and dark rum used in this filling. Combined with the sweet pineapple, which brightens the flavor, and toasted nuts, which add richness, this pie packs a lot of flavor.

Preheat the oven to 350°F.

In a large bowl, whisk together the butter, sugar, corn syrup, rum, vanilla, and eggs until well combined.

Spread the pineapple and chopped macadamia nuts evenly in the bottom of the pastry crust, then pour the egg mixture over the top. Tap the pie gently on the counter to release any air bubbles.

Place the pie on a baking sheet and bake for 50–60 minutes, or until the filling is puffed all over and set. Cool to room temperature before serving.

Honey Cardamom Banana Nut Pie

SERVES 8

3 ripe bananas, peeled and sliced ¼" thick

1 (9") Graham Pecan Crust (see Chapter 1), baked and cooled

1½ cups whole milk

¼ cup sugar

¼ cup honey

3 tablespoons cornstarch

½ teaspoon cardamom

1 egg

¼ teaspoon salt

2 tablespoons butter

1 teaspoon vanilla

1 recipe Stabilized Whipped Cream (see Chapter 2)

2 tablespoons toasted chopped pecans

Lightly citrus, yet charmingly earthy, cardamom is a wonderful baking spice that adds both beautiful flavor and aroma to this pie. It works especially well with honey and bananas, adding a little sharp edge to the sweet flavors. If you want to bump up this pie's nutty flavor profile, simply replace the regular butter with a couple of tablespoons of walnut, hazelnut, almond, or cashew butter. These butters will keep your custard smooth while still giving this pie an added layer of dimension.

Evenly layer the banana slices in the prepared crust. Set aside.

In a medium saucepan, combine the milk, sugar, honey, cornstarch, cardamom, egg, and salt. Whisk until smooth, then cook over medium heat, stirring constantly, until it begins to boil and thicken, about 10 minutes.

Remove from the heat and add the butter and vanilla. Stir until melted. Pour through a strainer into a separate bowl, then pour directly into the prepared crust. Place a layer of cling film directly on the custard, and chill overnight.

Once the pie has chilled, prepare the Stabilized Whipped Cream and top the pie. Garnish with the toasted pecans. Chill for 30 minutes before serving.

Brandied Black Cherry Pie

SERVES 8

20 ounces frozen pitted black cherries

¼ cup brandy

1 cup sugar

½ cup cornstarch

2 tablespoons butter

¼ teaspoon salt

1 teaspoon lemon juice

½ teaspoon vanilla

1 (9") Mealy Pie Crust (see Chapter 1), unbaked

1 recipe Flaky Pie Crust (see Chapter 1), cut into 10 (1") strips

1 egg, beaten

When baking with frozen fruit—like the beautiful black cherries found in this recipe—it is important to thoroughly thaw it before baking. As fruit thaws, it releases juice because the process of freezing damages the fruit's cells; if you skip the thaw you will find that your filling will be too wet. Draining off the excess juice will mean your filling will come out of the oven nice and thick!

Preheat the oven to 375°F.

Thaw the cherries and drain the juices into a measuring cup.

Add enough juice to the brandy to equal ½ cup. Add water if needed.

In a small saucepan over medium heat, combine the brandy mixture with the sugar and cornstarch until smooth. Cook, whisking constantly, until the mixture begins to boil and thicken, about 5 minutes. Remove the pot from the heat.

Add the butter, salt, lemon juice, and vanilla. Mix well, and then fold in the cherries. Cool to room temperature.

Pour into the Mealy Pie Crust and top with the pastry strips. Lay out 5 strips on top of the filling about ½" apart.

Starting ½" from the edge of the pie, fold back every other strip and lay down one strip of pastry. Fold the pastry back down and fold back the other pieces. Lay down a second strip about ½" from the fist strip. Repeat this process until all the strips are used.

Trim the dough to within 1" of the pan's edge. Tuck the edge of the top crust under the edge of the bottom crust. Crimp the dough using your fingers or a fork. Brush the lattice with beaten egg.

Bake for 40–45 minutes, or until the filling is bubbly in the center and the lattice is golden brown. Cool for 30 minutes before serving.

Pineapple Coconut Chess Pie

SERVES 8

4 eggs

1 stick butter, melted

1 cup sugar

1 tablespoon yellow corn meal

1 teaspoon vanilla

½ cup milk

¼ teaspoon coconut extract

½ cup toasted coconut

¼ cup crushed pineapple, drained

1 (9") Mealy Pie Crust (see Chapter 1), unbaked

Chess pie is a quintessentially southern creation. Most traditional chess pies are made of either lemon or chocolate, but the sweet, creamy filling is ripe for experimentation and exotic, unexpected flavors like the pineapple and coconut found in this recipe. If you're so inclined, a tablespoon of rum also makes a lovely addition to this pie filling.

Preheat the oven to 350°F.

In a large bowl, whisk together the eggs, butter, and sugar until smooth.

Add the cornmeal, vanilla, milk, and coconut extract. Whisk until well combined.

Spread the coconut and pineapple evenly over the bottom of the prepared crust. Pour the mixture into the pastry crust and place on a baking sheet.

Bake for 50–55 minutes, or until the filling is set and the top is golden brown. Allow to cool to room temperature before serving.

Bourbon Caramel Apple Pie

SERVES 8

¾ cup sugar

⅓ cup cornstarch

1 teaspoon cinnamon

½ teaspoon fresh-grated nutmeg

8 medium Granny Smith apples, peeled, cored, and sliced ⅛" thick

20 caramels

2 tablespoons bourbon

1 (9") Mealy Pie Crust (see Chapter 1), unbaked

1 egg, beaten

1 recipe Flaky Pie Crust (see Chapter 1), unbaked

Caramel and bourbon are quite complementary. Where bourbon is earthy, sharp, and smoky, caramel is sweet, buttery, and nutty. Combine those flavors with tart apple and you have a rich dessert that goes far beyond your plain, old apple pie! Before you think that this pie is going to taste heavy, remember the crisp, tart Granny Smith apples used in the filling. This hearty pie is perfect for the holidays!

Preheat the oven to 400°F.

In a large bowl, mix the sugar, cornstarch, cinnamon, and nutmeg until well blended. Add the apples and toss to coat. Allow to stand 10 minutes.

In a small saucepan over medium-low heat, add the caramels and bourbon. Heat until the mixture is thoroughly melted. Cool for 5 minutes.

Layer ⅓ of the apple mixture into the bottom of the Mealy Pie Crust, then drizzle ½ the caramel sauce over. Repeat, ending with a final layer of apples.

Brush the edge of the bottom pie crust with the beaten egg so the top crust will adhere. Top with the flaky crust and trim the dough to within 1" of the pan's edge. Tuck edge of the top crust under the edge of the bottom crust. Crimp the dough using your fingers or a fork. Brush the entire top crust with the beaten egg, and cut 4 or 5 slits in the top to vent steam.

Bake for 20 minutes, then reduce the heat to 350°F and cook for an additional 40–50 minutes, or until the filling is bubbling and the crust is golden brown all over. Cool for 1 hour before serving.

Brandied Berry Pie

SERVES 8

1 All-Butter Pie Crust (see Chapter 1), unbaked

2 cups fresh red cherries, pitted and sliced in half

1½ cups fresh blueberries

1½ cups fresh raspberries

1 cup sugar

¼ cup cornstarch

½ cup brandy

½ teaspoon cinnamon

1 teaspoon vanilla

¼ teaspoon salt

2 teaspoons lemon zest

1 recipe Oat Crumble (see Chapter 2)

Want to avoid the brandy? A lot of people, for various reasons, do not like to cook or bake with alcohol. If you are among those people don't worry, you can still enjoy this pie by making a couple of small substitutions. Simply replace the brandy with equal amounts of cherry, cranberry, or apple juice along with ¼ teaspoon almond or rum extract. The juice will add plenty of flavor, and the extract will add the depth this pie needs to take it from everyday to extraordinarily indulgent.

Preheat the oven to 375°F.

Line the pie crust with parchment paper or a double layer of aluminum foil and add pie weights or dry beans.

Bake for 10 minutes, then remove the paper and weights and bake for an additional 10–12 minutes, or until the crust is just turning golden brown all over. Remove from the oven and set aside to cool. Turn the oven up to 425°F.

In a large bowl, combine the cherries, blueberries, raspberries, sugar, and cornstarch until evenly distributed. Pour over the brandy along with the cinnamon, vanilla, salt, and lemon zest and stir to combine.

Pour the berry mixture into the prepared crust and top with the Oat Crumble. Place the pie on a baking sheet and bake for 15 minutes.

Reduce the heat to 350°F and bake for an additional 40–50 minutes, or until the filling is bubbling in the center and the Oat Crumble is crisp. Cool to room temperature before serving.

Strawberry Silk Pie

SERVES 8

1 Cream Cheese Pastry Crust (see Chapter 1), unbaked

1 cup strawberries, hulled and diced

2 tablespoons sugar

1 teaspoon cornstarch

1½ cups half-and-half

½ cup sugar

¼ cup cornstarch

2 eggs

¼ teaspoon salt

½ teaspoon vanilla

2 tablespoons butter

2 cups fresh strawberries, hulled and sliced in half

¼ cup apricot jam, melted and cooled

The silky, smooth strawberry custard found in this pie is made with perfectly puréed fresh strawberries that are cooked down to concentrate the flavor. Do not skip the cooling step between cooking the berries and puréeing. Hot foods expand when they are blended and can spray out of the blender; setting aside time for a brief cool-down will reduce that risk. It is also a good idea to vent the blender's lid whenever you purée warm foods.

Preheat the oven to 375°F. Line the pie crust with parchment paper or a double layer of aluminum foil, and add pie weights or dry beans.

Bake for 12 minutes, then remove the paper and weights and bake for an additional 12–15 minutes, or until the crust is golden brown all over. Remove from the oven and set aside to cool.

In a small pot, combine the strawberries and sugar. Let stand for 10 minutes, then cook over medium heat until they are thick and bubbling, about 10 minutes.

Remove from the heat and cool for 5 minutes, then pour the strawberry mixture into a blender and process until smooth.

Pour the strawberry purée through a fine metal strainer, working the mixture through with a spatula, to remove the seeds. Return the strained berries to the pan and whisk in the cornstarch. Cook over medium heat until the mixture comes to a boil and thickens, about 5 minutes. Remove the pan from the heat and allow to cool.

In a medium saucepan, combine the half-and-half, sugar, cornstarch, eggs, and salt. Whisk until smooth, then cook over medium heat, stirring constantly, until it begins to boil and thicken, about 10 minutes.

Remove from the heat and add the vanilla, butter, and strawberry mixture. Whisk until the butter is melted and the mixture is smooth. Pour through a strainer into a separate bowl, then pour directly into the prepared crust. Place a layer of cling film directly on the custard and chill for 2 hours.

Remove the cling film from the pie and arrange the strawberries, sliced-side down, on top of the custard. Brush the berries with the apricot jam. Serve chilled.

Green Tea Passion Fruit Mousse Pie

SERVES 8

3 teaspoons matcha green tea powder

2 tablespoons hot water

2 cups half-and-half

⅔ cup sugar

¼ cup passion fruit purée

¼ cup cornstarch

2 egg yolks

¼ teaspoon salt

½ teaspoon vanilla

2 tablespoons butter

1 recipe Stabilized Whipped Cream (see Chapter 2)

1 Traditional Graham Cracker Crust (see Chapter 1), baked and cooled

This pie uses a green tea powder called *matcha*, which is made from shade-grown green tea leaves that are steamed and then powdered. You'll find this flavoring in many Japanese desserts, ice cream, and western-style pastries. It can be found in some grocery stores as well as gourmet stores, and tea and coffee shops, or it can be purchased online.

In a small bowl, combine the green tea powder with the hot water and mix until smooth. Set aside to cool.

In a medium saucepan, combine the half-and-half, sugar, fruit purée, cornstarch, egg yolks, and salt. Whisk until smooth, then cook over medium heat, stirring constantly, until it begins to boil and thicken, about 8 minutes.

Remove from the heat and add the vanilla, butter, and green tea mixture. Whisk until the butter is melted and the mixture is smooth. Pour the custard through a strainer into a large bowl, cover with plastic, and cool to room temperature, about 1 hour.

Once cool, fold half the Stabilized Whipped Cream into the green tea base. Spread the filling into the prepared crust, cover with plastic, and chill for 2 hours.

Once the filling is cold, spread the remaining whipped cream over the top of the pie. Serve chilled.

Triple-Berry Cream Puff Pie

SERVES 8

½ cup water

¼ cup butter

¼ teaspoon salt

1 tablespoon sugar

½ cup all-purpose flour

2 eggs

1½ cups half-and-half

½ cup sugar

2 tablespoons cornstarch

2 eggs

¼ teaspoon salt

½ teaspoon vanilla

2 tablespoons butter

½ cup chopped fresh strawberries

½ cup fresh blueberries

½ cup fresh raspberries

1 recipe Stabilized Whipped Cream (see Chapter 2)

In place of a traditional pastry crust, this not-so-humble pie uses a base of *pate a choux*, a French pastry dough that is first cooked on the stove and then baked. It is the same dough used to make cream puffs and éclairs. The name literally translates into "little cabbages," due to the shape of the dough once it is baked. This pie is essentially an exquisite, inside-out cream puff topped with fresh ripe berries and whipped cream.

Preheat the oven to 400°F.

In a large saucepan, bring water, butter, salt, and sugar to a boil over medium heat. Add flour all at once and immediately beat the mixture with a spoon until it forms a smooth ball. Remove from the heat and allow to cool for 5 minutes.

Transfer the mixture to the work bowl of a stand mixer and add eggs, one at a time, beating well after each addition. Continue beating until mixture is smooth and shiny.

Spread the mixture onto the bottom and halfway up the sides of a 9" pie plate sprayed with nonstick cooking spray. Bake for 10 minutes, then reduce the heat to 350°F and bake for 15–25 minutes more, or until the dough is puffed, firm, and shiny. Cool completely on a wire rack.

In a medium saucepan, combine the half-and-half, sugar, cornstarch, eggs, and salt. Whisk until smooth, then cook over medium heat, stirring constantly, until it begins to boil and thicken, about 10 minutes.

Remove from the heat and add the vanilla and butter. Whisk until the butter is melted, then pour through a strainer into a separate bowl and place that bowl in an ice bath. Chill the custard, stirring constantly, until cool.

Spread the cool custard into the crust and arrange the berries on top. Spread the Stabilized Whipped Cream over the top, and chill for 1 hour before serving.

Apricot Macaroon Pie

SERVES 8

1 cup all-purpose flour

½ cup almond meal

1 cup packed light brown sugar

3 cups unsweetened shredded coconut

½ teaspoon salt

¾ cup butter, melted and cooled

4 egg whites

1 pound fresh apricots, peeled, pitted, and diced

¼ cup sugar

2 tablespoons cornstarch

¼ teaspoon cinnamon

This pie has a unique crust and a topping that is full of flavor: Here, ground almonds and coconut are combined to create a flavor that is similar to the popular cookie, but in pie form. The topping looks particularly pretty when some bits of the apricot stick out, so do not be too precise when covering the fruit filling.

Preheat the oven to 350°F.

In a large bowl, combine the flour, ¼ cup of the almond meal, ½ cup of the sugar, 1 cup of the coconut, and salt. Whisk to combine, then pour in the melted butter.

Mix until the dough is clumping together; it will not form a smooth ball. Press the mixture into a 9" pie pan and bake for 15–20 minutes, or until firm and lightly golden. Remove from the oven and set aside to cool. Leave the oven on.

In a medium bowl, combine the remaining almond meal, sugar, and coconut with the egg whites. Mix until well combined.

In a medium pot, combine the apricots, sugar, cornstarch, and cinnamon. Mix until well coated. Cook over medium heat until the mixture is thick and bubbling, about 8–10 minutes. Remove from the heat and allow to cool for 10 minutes.

Pour the apricot mixture into the prepared crust and top with the coconut mixture. Bake for 25–30 minutes, or until the topping is deeply golden and the fruit is bubbling. Cool for 1 hour before serving.

Chapter 5

Tarts, Tartlets, and Rustic Pies

Tarts are elegant. They can be made in nearly any shape or size you can imagine. And whether you fill your tart with Gorgonzola, fig, tarragon, rose, quince, or any other upscale ingredient it is a delicious and gourmet alternative to the traditional pie.

What makes a tart different from a pie is the crust; there is a lower filling-to-crust ratio, making the tart the place for a favorite crust to shine. A tart crust is typically made from short crust pastry, which, for sweet pies, means that the crust is like a sophisticated shortbread cookie, buttery and crumbly. However, if you have a favorite pie pastry, you can use that, too! With tarts—as with pie—the only rule is to make something you love.

Ginger Pear Tart

SERVES 8

4 Bosc pears, peeled, cored, and sliced ¼" thick

1 teaspoon fresh-grated ginger

½ cup packed light brown sugar

¼ teaspoon cinnamon

1 tablespoon cornstarch

½ cup crushed gingersnap cookies

2 tablespoons butter, melted

1 (12") All-Butter Pie Crust (see Chapter 1), chilled

Spicy ginger is delicious with all kinds of fruits, but it is especially delicious when combined with the succulent flavor of fresh ripe pears. For a bit of extra ginger kick, and a trendy rustic look, this tart is topped with a buttery gingersnap cookie crumble. Add a little vanilla ice cream for the perfect final flourish.

Preheat the oven to 425°F. Line a baking sheet with parchment paper.

In a large bowl, combine the pears, ginger, brown sugar, cinnamon, and cornstarch. Toss until the fruit is evenly coated, then set aside for 5 minutes.

In a small bowl, combine the gingersnap crumbs with the butter until the crumbs are evenly coated.

Place the pastry on the prepared baking sheet. Arrange the pears on the pastry, leaving a 2" border. Pour any juices over the top. Carefully fold the pastry over the pears, then spread the gingersnap crumbs over the top.

Bake for 10 minutes, then reduce the heat to 350°F and bake for an additional 30–40 minutes, or until the pastry is golden and the fruit is tender. Cool to room temperature before serving.

Pear Gorgonzola Tart

SERVES 8

3 Bosc pears, peeled, cored, and sliced ¼" thick

¼ teaspoon cayenne pepper

1 (12") Lard Crust (see Chapter 1), chilled

2 ounces cream cheese, room temperature

¼ cup fig jam

2 ounces Gorgonzola cheese, crumbled

Gorgonzola, an enchanting blue cheese produced in the northern part of Italy, has a pungent flavor that gives this indulgent pie a distinct bite. However, while distinct, this bite doesn't overwhelm the dish; rather, it's tempered by the addition of sweet pears and fig jam. For the best flavor, this tart should be served slightly warm.

Preheat the oven to 425°F. Line a baking sheet with parchment paper.

In a large bowl, combine the pears and cayenne pepper until evenly coated. Set aside.

Place the pastry crust on the prepared baking sheet. Spread the cream cheese in the center of the pastry, leaving a 2" border around the edge.

Spread the fig jam over the top of the cream cheese, then arrange the pear slices over the top. Carefully fold the edges of the pastry over the fruit and top with the crumbled Gorgonzola cheese.

Bake for 10 minutes, then reduce the heat to 350°F and bake for an additional 30–40 minutes, or until the pastry is golden brown and the fruit is tender. Serve slightly warm.

Fig Tart

SERVES 8

¾ cup mascarpone cheese

2 teaspoons orange zest

1 teaspoon vanilla

3 tablespoons honey

2 tablespoons sugar

1 egg yolk

¼ teaspoon salt

1 (10") Cornmeal Tart Crust (see Chapter 1), chilled

2 tablespoons apricot jam

10 mission figs, quartered

Fresh ripe figs are tasty all on their own, but when you place them atop a tart filled with a lightly sweet lemon mascarpone filling, they become irresistible! The figs are front and center, and in this recipe they are not cooked, to preserve their delicate flavor. Be sure to buy fresh ripe figs and use them within a day or two of buying for the best flavor.

In a large bowl, whisk together the mascarpone, orange zest, vanilla, honey, sugar, egg yolk, and salt. Cover and chill for 30 minutes.

Preheat the oven to 350°F.

Spread the mascarpone mixture onto the molded pastry. Bake for 25–35 minutes, or until the crust is golden brown and the cheese filling has just set. Cool to room temperature.

In a small bowl, add the apricot jam. Heat in the microwave in 10-second bursts, until the jam is melted.

To serve, top the tart with the sliced figs and brush the jam over the figs. Serve immediately.

Fig Tart

Torta della Nonna (Italian Cheese Tart)

SERVES 8

4 egg yolks

¾ cup sugar

⅔ cup all-purpose flour

1 tablespoon orange zest

2 cups milk

1½ cups ricotta cheese

¼ cup pine nuts

1 (10") Short Crust for Tarts (see Chapter 1), unbaked and untrimmed

1 All-Butter Pie Crust (see Chapter 1), rolled into a 12" circle

1 egg, beaten

Powdered sugar, for garnish

The name of this Tuscan recipe means "Grandmother's tart." But with this pie's creamy ricotta cheese, orange zest, and pine nuts, your grandmother wouldn't know what to do with this upscale Torta della Nonna. This tart can be made up to a day before baking.

Preheat the oven to 375°F.

In the bowl of a double boiler, whisk together the egg yolks and sugar until smooth.

Gradually whisk in the flour so there are no lumps, then whisk in the orange zest.

Stream in the milk, whisking constantly, until smooth.

Heat the double boiler until the water simmers. Cook, stirring constantly, until the custard thickens. Remove from the heat and stir in the ricotta cheese and pine nuts.

Spread the filling into the Short Crust. Lay the All-Butter Pie Crust over the top and use the edge of the pan to trim off any excess. Pinch the edges of the crust together by pressing your thumb against the side of the tart pan, and brush the top of the crust with beaten egg.

Place the tart on a baking sheet and bake for 50–55 minutes, or until the tart is golden brown. Cool to room temperature, and dust with powdered sugar before serving.

White Chocolate Ganache Tart with Brûléed Bananas

SERVES 8

⅓ cup heavy whipping cream

1 cup white chocolate, finely chopped

¼ cup powdered sugar

3 ounces cream cheese, room temperature

½ teaspoon vanilla

1 Brown Butter–Graham Cracker Tart Crust (see Chapter 1), baked and cooled

2 medium bananas, cut into ¼" thick slices

3 tablespoons sugar

The slight tang from the cream cheese gives this tart an incredibly rich flavor that pairs well with the sweet flavor of bananas and deeply caramelized sugar, but the flavor profile isn't the only thing that makes this pie amazing. To give your guests a little show, brûlée this tart just before serving.

In a small saucepan over medium heat, cook the cream until it simmers. Remove the pot from the heat and add the chopped chocolate. Let the mixture stand for 1 minute, then whisk until smooth. Set aside to cool to room temperature.

In the bowl of a stand mixer or in a large bowl with a hand mixer, add the powdered sugar, cream cheese, and vanilla. Beat the mixture until smooth.

Add in the ganache and whip until lighter in texture. Pour into the prepared tart crust, cover with plastic wrap, and chill for at least 4 hours, or overnight.

Once the filling has chilled, cover the top with the sliced bananas and sprinkle the sugar evenly over the top. Under the broiler or with a kitchen torch, melt the sugar until it turns an amber color. Chill for 5 minutes in the refrigerator before serving.

Toasted Almond, Coconut, and Chocolate Tart

SERVES 8

1 (10") Short Crust for Tarts (see Chapter 1), unbaked

½ cup milk

3 tablespoons butter, softened

1 tablespoon all-purpose flour

½ cup sugar

1 egg

¼ teaspoon salt

1 teaspoon vanilla

1 cup sweetened shredded coconut

⅓ cup slivered almonds, toasted

¼ cup heavy cream

1 tablespoon butter

4 ounces semisweet chocolate, chopped

Toasted coconut and toasted slivered almonds, to garnish

This tart is inspired by the popular coconut and almond candy bar, but it has a much more grown-up feel. Hidden under a glossy layer of chocolate ganache is a soft coconut and almond custard that is jam-packed with sophisticated and succulent flavor. It is both beautiful and, if you are a coconut lover, absolutely irresistible.

Preheat the oven to 350°F.

Line the tart with parchment paper or a double layer of aluminum foil and add pie weights or dry beans.

Bake for 10 minutes, then remove the paper and weights and bake for an additional 10–12 minutes, or until the crust is lightly golden brown all over. Remove from the oven and set aside to cool. Leave the oven on.

In a medium saucepan, bring the milk to a simmer over medium heat. Remove from the heat and cool slightly.

In a large bowl, whisk together the butter, flour, and sugar until well combined. Add the egg and beat well.

Slowly pour in the milk, whisking constantly, then add the salt and vanilla. Fold in the coconut and toasted almonds.

Pour the mixture into the prepared pastry crust and place on a sheet pan. Bake in the lower third of the oven for 10 minutes, then reduce the heat to 325°F and bake for an additional 25–35 minutes, or until the filling is set at the edges and just slightly wobbly in the center. Cool for 1 hour before making the topping.

In a small saucepan, bring the cream to a bare simmer. Remove from the heat and add the butter and chocolate. Let stand 1 minute, then whisk until smooth.

Cool the mixture for 10 minutes, then carefully spread over the pie. Garnish with toasted coconut and almonds. Chill until the topping is set, about 1 hour.

Vanilla Bean and Saffron Poached Pear Tart

SERVES 8

1 recipe Blitz Puff Pastry (see Chapter 1)

1 cup sugar

½ teaspoon saffron threads

1 vanilla bean, split and seeds scraped out

4 Bosc pears, peeled, sliced in half, and cored

½ cup half-and-half

3 tablespoons sugar

1 tablespoon cornstarch

1 egg yolk

1 teaspoon vanilla

2 tablespoons butter

Powdered sugar, for garnish

Saffron, the world's most expensive spice, is an indulgent ingredient, but it is well worth the expense. Nothing compares to saffron's one-of-a-kind flavor or the lovely orange color it imparts. This tart features tender pears poached in saffron-infused syrup. Reserve the poaching syrup for iced tea or cocktails.

Preheat the oven to 400°F. Line a baking sheet with parchment paper. Roll the pastry out to ¼" thick and trim into a 12" square. Place the pastry on the prepared baking sheet and dock with a fork. Top the pastry with a second sheet of parchment paper, and then place a second baking sheet on top of the pastry.

Bake for 12–15 minutes, or until the pastry is firm, then remove the top baking sheet and parchment paper and bake for an additional 12–15 minutes, or until the pastry is golden brown and crisp. Allow to cool completely to room temperature.

In a large saucepan over medium heat, combine 4 cups of water with the sugar, saffron threads, vanilla bean, and vanilla seeds. Carefully add the pears and cover with a sheet of parchment paper with a small hole cut in the center. Simmer the pears until tender, 15–25 minutes. A paring knife will slide easily in and out of the pear when it is ready. Remove the pan from the heat and allow the pears to cool in their liquid.

In a medium saucepan over medium heat, whisk together the half-and-half, sugar, cornstarch, and egg yolk until the mixture thickens and starts to boil, about 10 minutes.

Remove the pan from the heat and add the vanilla and butter. Whisk until completely incorporated. Pour the mixture through a strainer, then into a bowl. Place a layer of cling film directly on the custard and chill for at least 2 hours.

To assemble the tart, begin by spreading the vanilla custard evenly over the puff pastry crust, leaving a ½" border around the edges. With a sharp paring knife, slice the bottom of the pear downward into ¼" slices, leaving the top of the pear intact. Lay the pears onto the custard and gently press the sliced end to fan out the fruit. Chill the tart for 1 hour. Dust with powdered sugar just before serving.

Praline Crème Tart with Mocha Whipped Cream

SERVES 8

1¼ cups milk

⅓ cup light brown sugar

2 tablespoons cornstarch

1 egg yolk

¼ cup hazelnut butter

1 teaspoon vanilla

2 tablespoons butter

1 teaspoon dry gelatin

2 tablespoons cold espresso

1 pint heavy whipping cream, cold

¼ cup powdered sugar

1 tablespoon Dutch-processed cocoa powder, plus extra for garnish

Praline is a word that describes sweet nut confections. Most people think of the praline candy, but the word encompasses so much more. In this case, the nut used is hazelnut, which is ground into butter and then cooked into a creamy custard. It is topped with a mocha whipped cream to add an extra layer of indulgence.

In a medium saucepan over medium heat, whisk together the milk, sugar, cornstarch, and egg yolk until the mixture starts to get warm. Add the hazelnut butter and whisk until it thickens and starts to starts to boil, about 10 minutes.

Remove the pan from the heat and add the vanilla and butter. Whisk until completely incorporated. Pour the mixture through a strainer, then into the prepared crust. Place a layer of cling film directly on the custard and chill for at least 6 hours, or overnight.

Once the pie is chilled, prepare the whipped cream. Combine the gelatin and the cold espresso. Allow to stand for 5 minutes, or until completely bloomed. Heat for five seconds in the microwave, making sure it is completely melted, then cool to room temperature.

Pour the cold cream into a large bowl. Add the powdered sugar and cocoa powder. Whip on medium-low speed until the sugar and cocoa are blended, then increase the speed to medium-high.

When the cream is softly whipped, pour in the cooled gelatin. Whip until the cream forms medium peaks, about 2 minutes. Spread on top of the chilled pie. Chill for 30 minutes before serving.

Homemade Ricotta and Berry Compote Tart

SERVES 8

1 (10") Short Crust for Tarts (see Chapter 1), unbaked

2 quarts whole milk

1 cup heavy cream

½ teaspoon salt

3 tablespoons fresh lemon juice

3 cups mixed fresh berries (use whatever combination of fresh berries you like best)

¼ cup sugar

¼ teaspoon cinnamon

½ teaspoon vanilla

2 tablespoons honey

Nothing compares to the flavor and richness of homemade ricotta cheese, which perfectly complements the sweet and tangy mixed berry compote spread on top. Happily, it is easy to make your own cheese, and everyone will be impressed by your not-so-humble pie—and by you!

Preheat the oven to 350°F.

Line the tart with parchment paper or a double layer of aluminum foil and add pie weights or dry beans. Bake for 12 minutes, then remove the paper and weights and bake for an additional 10–15 minutes, or until the crust is golden brown all over. Remove from the oven and set aside to cool. Leave the oven on.

In a large pot over medium-high, add the milk, cream, and salt. Bring the mixture to a rolling boil, stirring occasionally to prevent scorching.

Once the mixture reaches a boil, add the lemon juice, then reduce the heat to low and simmer, stirring constantly, until the mixture curdles, about 2 minutes.

Line a strainer with 2 layers of cheese cloth. Pour the mixture into the lined strainer and allow the cheese to drain 1 hour.

In a medium pot, combine the berries, sugar, and cinnamon. Cook the fruit over medium heat, stirring occasionally, until the berries are softened and the sugar is dissolved, about 8 minutes. Remove the pot from the heat and stir in the vanilla. Cool to room temperature.

In a small bowl, combine 1 cup of the fresh ricotta with the honey until well mixed. Carefully spread the ricotta mixture into the bottom of the prepared tart crust. Spoon the berry compote over the top. Serve slightly chilled or at room temperature.

Grilled Peach Puff Pastry Tart

SERVES 8

1 recipe Blitz Puff Pastry
(see Chapter 1)

8 peaches, sliced in half and
the pit removed

4 ounces cream cheese,
room temperature

2 tablespoons golden syrup
or honey

¼ cup powdered sugar, plus
more for garnish

½ teaspoon vanilla bean
paste or vanilla

1 teaspoon lemon zest

Do you ever find yourself with peaches that are just a little too hard to eat raw? Put them on the grill to make them lusciously soft with a slightly caramelized flavor. Here, these sumptuous grilled peaches rest atop honey-sweetened cream cheese and crispy puff pastry.

Preheat the oven to 400°F. Line a baking sheet with parchment paper.

Roll the pastry out to ¼" thick and trim into a 12" square. Place the pastry on the prepared baking sheet and dock with a fork. Top the pastry with a second sheet of parchment paper, and then place a second baking sheet on top of the pastry.

Bake for 12–15 minutes, or until the pastry is firm, then remove the top baking sheet and parchment paper and bake for an additional 12–15 minutes, or until the pastry is golden brown and crisp. Allow to cool completely to room temperature.

Heat the grill or an indoor grill pan to medium heat. Once hot, oil the grate so the fruit will not stick.

Place the peaches flesh-side down and grill for 2–3 minutes, or until the peaches easily release from the grill and have light grill marks. Flip the peaches and cook skin-side down for 1–2 more minutes, or until the peaches are soft. Remove from the grill and cool to room temperature. Remove the peach skin; it will be easy to peel off after grilling.

In a medium bowl, combine the cream cheese, golden syrup, powdered sugar, vanilla beans, and lemon zest. Whisk until the cream cheese is smooth and lighter in texture.

Spread the cream cheese mixture over the puff pastry, leaving a ½" border around the edge. Arrange the peach halves over the top. Dust with powdered sugar just before serving.

Pumpkin Rum Mousse Tart

SERVES 8

1 cup cream

1 (15-ounce) can pumpkin purée

1 cup packed light brown sugar

¾ teaspoon kosher salt

½ teaspoon ground cinnamon

¼ teaspoon ground nutmeg

3 egg yolks

2 tablespoons spiced rum

2 teaspoons gelatin

3 tablespoons cold water

½ teaspoon vanilla

2 tablespoons sugar

1 (10") Brown Butter–Graham Cracker Crust (see Chapter 1), baked and cooled

½ recipe Spiked Whipped Cream (see Chapter 2), made with spiced rum

This tart takes your run-of-the mill pumpkin pie and, using a rum-laced pumpkin mousse and a sophisticated presentation, turns it into an autumnal delight that no one will forget. The mousse is beautifully light but with a rich flavor, and presents your palate with a symphony of spiced pumpkin bliss!

In a double boiler, heat ½ cup of cream, pumpkin, brown sugar, salt, cinnamon, nutmeg, egg yolks, and rum until hot, about 10–12 minutes, or until the mixture has thickened. Remove from the heat.

Dissolve the gelatin in the cold water and add to the hot pumpkin mixture; mix well. Allow the mixture to cool to room temperature.

In a medium bowl, whip the remaining heavy cream with an electric mixer or in the work bowl of a stand mixer until it forms soft peaks, about 1½ minutes.

Add the sugar and continue to beat until you have firm peaks, about 1 minute more. Fold the whipped cream into the cooled pumpkin mixture, then pour it into the prepared tart crust. Chill for 2 hours, or overnight. Serve with Spiked Whipped Cream.

Strawberry White Chocolate Ganache Tart

SERVES 8

¼ cup heavy cream

12 ounces white chocolate, coarsely chopped

½ teaspoon vanilla

4 ounces cream cheese, room temperature

1 (10") Brown Butter–Graham Cracker Crust (see Chapter 1), baked and cooled

2 cups fresh strawberries, stemmed and thinly sliced

2 tablespoons powdered sugar

Fresh strawberries and white chocolate are a popular combination, especially when you're looking to add a sensual air to your dessert. This tart takes that combination to the limit with a thick white chocolate ganache filling topped with slices of fresh berries. The crust for this tart is made with toasty brown butter to deepen the tart's seductive flavor.

In a medium saucepan over medium heat, add the cream and heat until it simmers. Remove the pan from the heat and add the chopped chocolate and vanilla. Let stand for 1 minute, then whisk until smooth.

In the bowl of a stand mixer or in a large bowl with an electric mixer beat together the white chocolate ganache and cream cheese until smooth.

Pour the ganache carefully into the prepared crust. Cool on the counter for 2 hours, then chill for 2 hours. Once chilled, arrange the sliced strawberries on the top of the tart. Dust with powdered sugar just before serving.

Fresh Blackberry Tart with Spiked Crème Anglaise

SERVES 8

2 cups fresh blackberries

2 tablespoons cornstarch

2 tablespoons sugar

1 Short Crust for Tarts (see Chapter 1) rolled into a 12" circle

1 tablespoon butter

½ cup heavy cream

1 teaspoon vanilla bean paste

1 tablespoon bourbon

2 egg yolks

3 tablespoons sugar

Crème anglaise is a slightly thickened custard sauce that is used as a garnish on all sorts of desserts. Here, the sauce is spiked with a little bourbon and drizzled over slices of warm blackberry tart. If you don't care for bourbon, you can use rum or crème de cassis in the crème anglaise or omit the alcohol altogether.

Preheat the oven to 400°F. Line a baking sheet with parchment paper.

In a medium bowl, combine the berries, cornstarch, and sugar until well combined. Let stand for 5 minutes.

Place the pastry on the prepared baking sheet. Spread the blackberry mixture onto the pastry, leaving a ½" border. Fold the pastry just over the edge of the berries, then dot the top with the butter.

Bake for 45–55 minutes, or until the fruit is bubbling and the pastry is golden brown. Remove from the oven and allow to cool slightly.

In a small saucepan over medium-low heat, add the cream and vanilla. Bring just to a simmer.

In a large bowl, whisk together the bourbon, egg yolks, and sugar until smooth. Whisking constantly, gradually add ½ cup of hot cream into egg yolks. Immediately add the egg yolk mixture back to the pot and cook, whisking constantly, until the mixture coats the back of a spoon, about 6 minutes.

Serve the tart slightly warm with the crème anglaise drizzled over the top.

Sour Cream Ganache Tart

SERVES 8

2 cups semisweet chocolate chips

1 cup sour cream

2 tablespoons cream

1 teaspoon vanilla

1 (10") Brown Butter–Graham Cracker Crust (see Chapter 1), baked and cooled

1 cup chopped strawberries

1 tablespoon sugar

In addition to giving the chocolate ganache filling in this recipe a tangy bite that keeps it from being too sweet, the sour cream provides the ganache with a silky soft texture that feels like velvet on the tongue. Fresh fruit or a fruit sauce would be a lovely garnish for this tart. If you like, you can also make this with white chocolate.

In a medium heat-proof bowl over the top of a pan of barely simmering water, add the chocolate. Heat until melted and smooth, stirring occasionally. Remove the bowl from the water.

Add the sour cream, cream, and vanilla to the chocolate and, with an electric mixer, beat the mixture until it is smooth. Immediately pour the mixture into the prepared crust and smooth the top. Chill for 4 hours.

In a small bowl, combine the strawberries and sugar. Allow to stand for 10 minutes. Serves slices of the tart with the strawberry mixture spooned over the top.

Bourbon Peach Tart

SERVES 8

5 peaches, pceled, pitted, and cut into ½" thick slices

¼ cup sugar

3 tablespoons cornstarch

2 tablespoons bourbon

⅛ teaspoon nutmeg

1 (10") Short Crust for Tarts (see Chapter 1), unbaked

Sour Cream Topping

The flavors of charred oak, caramel, and vanilla make bourbon a natural for sweet desserts. Those flavors help elevate the flavors of this humble peach tart into something really special. If you prefer, you can also use dark rum or brandy, which also have those lush smoky notes, or omit the alcohol altogether and use peach nectar for a little extra peach flavor.

Preheat the oven to 350°F.

In a large bowl, combine the peaches with the sugar, cornstarch, bourbon, and nutmeg. Let stand for 10 minutes.

Pour the peaches into the prepared crust and place the tart pan on a baking sheet. Bake for 45–55 minutes, or until the fruit is bubbling and the crust is golden brown. Cool to room temperature. Serve with Sour Cream Topping.

Apricot Tart with a Coconut Crumble

SERVES 8

15 fresh apricots, pitted and sliced ¼" thick

¾ cup sugar

⅓ cup cornstarch

¼ teaspoon cinnamon

⅓ cup all-purpose flour

¼ cup unsweetened coconut

½ cup sugar

¼ teaspoon salt

⅓ cup unsalted butter, cubed and chilled

1 (10") Short Crust for Tarts (see Chapter 1), unbaked

The unsweetened coconut in this recipe gives this chic crumble topping a little extra crispness without making it too sweet for the fresh apricots underneath, which is what sweetened coconut would do. This tart is perfect with a little fresh whipped cream or a scoop of ice cream on a warm day!

Preheat the oven to 375°F.

In a large bowl, combine the apricots, sugar, cornstarch, and cinnamon. Toss gently until all the fruit is evenly coated. Allow to stand for 10 minutes.

In a bowl, blend the flour, coconut, sugar, and salt. Using your fingers, rub in the butter until the mixture resembles coarse sand.

Pour the apricot mixture into the prepared tart shell and top with the coconut crumble. Bake for 40–45 minutes, or until the filling is bubbly in the center and the crumble is golden brown. Cool for 30 minutes before serving.

Black Cherry Meringue Tart

SERVES 8

1 (10") Short Crust for Tarts (see Chapter 1), unbaked

3 cups pitted black cherries

½ cup sugar

1 teaspoon vanilla

1 tablespoon amaretto or lemon juice

¼ cup cornstarch

1 recipe Fool-proof Meringue (see Chapter 2)

With a sharp taste and a deep red color, these black cherries are perfect for making a decadent dessert that is not too sweet. To balance the heavy cherry flavor of the filling, this tart is topped with a light and toasty meringue. To ensure that your pie looks as upscale as it tastes, use a large star tip to pipe "kisses" of meringue onto the tart.

Preheat the oven to 350°F.

Line the tart with parchment paper or a double layer of aluminum foil and add pie weights or dry beans. Bake for 10 minutes, then remove the paper and weights and bake for an additional 10–12 minutes, or until the crust is just golden brown all over. Remove from the oven and set aside to cool. Leave the oven on.

In a large bowl, combine the cherries, sugar, vanilla, amaretto, and cornstarch. Toss gently until all the fruit is evenly coated. Allow to stand for 10 minutes.

Pour the cherry mixture into the prepared tart shell and bake for 40–45 minutes, or until the filling is bubbly in the center.

Spread or pipe the meringue onto the hot cherry filling and return the tart to the oven until the meringue is golden brown, about 8–10 minutes. Allow the tart to come completely to room temperature before serving.

Caramel Pineapple Tart

SERVES 8

1 (10") Short Crust for Tarts (see Chapter 1), unbaked

1 large ripe pineapple, peeled, cut in half lengthwise, cored, and cut into ½" pieces

½ cup packed light brown sugar

1 tablespoon corn syrup

2 tablespoons dark rum

1 vanilla bean, split and seeds scraped out

Salted Caramel Sauce (see Chapter 2), for garnish

The firm texture and tangy flavor of fresh pineapple simply can't be beat, and the natural form of this delicious fruit is less sweet than canned versions. In this tart, the pineapple is cooked in a brown sugar and rum syrup until it is very tender, then it is spread into a crisp tart crust and topped with a little salted caramel sauce for a little extra caramel flavor.

Preheat the oven to 350°F.

Line the tart with parchment paper or a double layer of aluminum foil and add pie weights or dry beans. Bake for 10 minutes, then remove the paper and weights and bake for an additional 12–15 minutes, or until the crust is golden brown all over. Remove from the oven and set aside to cool. Leave the oven on.

In a large pot over medium heat, combine the pineapple, sugar, corn syrup, dark rum, and vanilla bean with seeds and cook until the pineapple is very tender and the liquid is very thick, about 30 minutes. Remove the pot from the heat and cool slightly.

Spoon the pineapple mixture into the prepared tart shell. Drizzle the tart with Salted Caramel Sauce. Serve at room temperature.

Apple Rose Tart

SERVES 8

1 (10") Short Crust for Tarts (see Chapter 1), unbaked

6 Granny Smith apples, peeled, cored, and cut ⅛" thick

¼ cup sugar

½ teaspoon cinnamon

1 tablespoon lemon juice

2 tablespoons cornstarch

2 tablespoons butter

1 tablespoon rose syrup or rose water

2 tablespoons apricot jam, melted and cooled

This epicurean apple tart goes above and beyond the traditional apple pie. It's flavored with delicately floral rose syrup, which is made from distilled rose essence. But while the taste of this tart is unrivaled, this dramatic tart is as beautiful to look at as it is to devour. For an impossible-to-resist presentation, arrange the thinly sliced apples so that they look like a rose with its petals unfurled.

Preheat the oven to 350°F.

Line the tart with parchment paper or a double layer of aluminum foil and add pie weights or dry beans. Bake for 10 minutes, then remove the paper and weights and bake for an additional 10–12 minutes, or until the crust is golden brown all over. Remove from the oven and set aside to cool. Turn the oven to 400°F.

In a large bowl, combine the apples, sugar, cinnamon, and lemon juice. Allow to stand for 30 minutes at room temperature. Drain the mixture, reserving the juices in a separate bowl. Toss the drained apples with the cornstarch and set aside.

In a small saucepan, combine the reserved apple juices with the butter and rose water. Cook the mixture, stirring often, over medium heat until it is reduced to ¼ cup, about 15–20 minutes. Pour the syrup over the apples and toss to coat.

Arrange the apple slices in overlapping concentric circles in the tart crust, starting at the edge and working toward the inside.

Bake the tart for 25–30 minutes, or until the apples are tender. Cool to room temperature, then brush the apricot jam over the fruit before serving.

Blueberry Ricotta Tart

SERVES 8

1 cup ricotta cheese

2 teaspoons lemon zest

1 teaspoon vanilla

2 tablespoons honey

2 tablespoons sugar

1 egg yolk

¼ teaspoon salt

1 (12") Short Crust for Tarts
(see Chapter 1), chilled

1 cup fresh blueberries

½ recipe Butter Crumble
(see Chapter 2)

Ricotta cheese has a mild flavor and a delicate texture that is perfect for serving alongside fresh fruit. Here, the ricotta adds an almost cheesecake-like layer, that acts as a flavorful backdrop for the honey and fresh lemon zest.

In a large bowl, whisk together the ricotta, lemon zest, vanilla, honey, sugar, egg yolk, and salt. Cover and chill for 30 minutes.

Preheat the oven to 350°F. Line a baking sheet with parchment paper.

Place the chilled pastry on the prepared baking sheet. Spread the ricotta mixture onto the pastry leaving a ½" border. Arrange the berries over the ricotta mixture, then fold the pastry just over the edge of the filling. Top with the Butter Crumble.

Bake for 45–55 minutes, or until the fruit is bubbling and both the crumble and pastry are golden brown. Cool to room temperature before serving.

Quince Tart Tatin

SERVES 8

1 recipe Blitz Puff Pastry (see Chapter 1)

½ cup sugar

¼ cup butter

6 quince, peeled, cored, and quartered

Fresh quince is very, very sour, and for that reason it cannot be eaten raw. Once cooked, however, the quince unveils its true nature. Its flesh takes on a delicate rose hue, and the flavor—which is similar to that of an apple crossed with a pear—becomes beautifully sweet. It is best to use fresh quince, which are available during the fall.

Preheat the oven to 400°F. Roll out the pastry until it is ⅛" thick and 12" wide. Cover with plastic and chill until ready to use.

In a 10" oven-proof skillet, add the sugar and water. Cook over medium heat, swirling occasionally but not stirring, until the sugar becomes golden-amber colored, about 6–7 minutes. Add the butter and swirl until melted.

Carefully place the quince, cheek-side down, into the pan as tightly as you can. Cook for 12–18 minutes, or until the quince have started to soften and the juices are thick. Remove the pan from the heat.

Place the pastry on top of the quince and carefully tuck edges around the quince with a butter knife.

Bake for 25–35 minutes, or until the crust is golden brown and firm to the touch. Remove from the oven and cool on a rack about 5 minutes before carefully turning out onto a serving plate.

Raspberry Curd Tart

SERVES 8

10 ounces fresh raspberries, plus more for garnish

2 tablespoons lemon juice

½ cup butter

¼ cup sugar

4 eggs

1 Chocolate Cookie Crust (see Chapter 1), baked in a 10" tart pan and cooled

1 recipe Stabilized Whipped Cream (see Chapter 2)

Fresh raspberry curd is what makes this dish delectable. Like lemon curd, it is silky, rich, and smooth, but rather than a sharp citrus tang it has the sweet, mild flavor of raspberries. If you find your raspberry curd is not as vibrantly pink as you would like, a drop or two of red food coloring will perk things up a bit.

In the work bowl of a food processor or blender, add the raspberries and lemon juice. Process until the mixture is smooth. Pour the raspberry purée through a strainer to remove the seeds.

In a medium saucepan over medium heat, add the raspberry purée along with the butter, sugar, and eggs. Whisk until smooth, then cook until thickened, about 12 minutes. Strain the raspberry mixture into a separate bowl, then spread into the prepared crust. Cover with plastic and chill for 4 hours.

Once chilled, prepare the Stabilized Whipped Cream and spread over the top of the tart. Garnish with fresh raspberries. Chill for 30 minutes before serving.

Lemon Pistachio Tart

SERVES 8

1 Lemon and Lavender Short Crust Pastry (see Chapter 1), unbaked

¼ cup salted pistachio nuts, plus more for garnish

3 tablespoons granulated sugar

1 tablespoon water

⅓ cup granulated sugar

2 tablespoons cornstarch

1¼ cups whole milk

2 egg yolks, lightly beaten

1 tablespoon lemon zest, plus more for garnish

¼ teaspoon kosher salt

¼ cup fresh lemon juice

1 tablespoon butter

¼ teaspoon vanilla

1 recipe Stabilized Whipped Cream (see Chapter 2)

This trendsetting tart uses pistachios and lemon to make a custard filling that elevates the humble nut into something divine. Pistachios have a naturally rich, buttery flavor, and the lemon in this recipe cuts that richness and adds a burst of fresh, clean flavor.

Preheat the oven to 350°F.

Line the Lemon and Lavender Short Crust Pastry with parchment paper or a double layer of aluminum foil and add pie weights or dry beans. Bake for 10 minutes, then remove the paper and weights and bake for an additional 10–12 minutes, or until the crust is lightly golden brown all over. Remove from the oven and set aside to cool.

In a food processor or blender, add the pistachios and pulse until the nuts are in small pieces but not a powder. Add in the sugar and water and pulse to combine.

In a medium saucepan, whisk together the pistachio paste, sugar, cornstarch, milk, egg yolks, lemon zest, and salt and whisk until smooth. Cook over medium heat until boiling and thickened.

Remove the pan from the heat and stir in the lemon juice, butter, and vanilla. Pour the mixture through a strainer into a large bowl, then pour into the prepared crust. Cover the tart with plastic and refrigerate for 4 hours.

Once chilled, decorate the tart with the Stabilized Whipped Cream. Garnish with additional ground pistachios and lemon zest.

Honey Tarragon Peach Tart

SERVES 8

5 peaches, peeled, pitted, and cut into ½" thick slices

2 tablespoons sugar

2 tablespoons honey

3 tablespoons cornstarch

2 teaspoons freshly chopped tarragon

1 (10") Short Crust for Tarts (see Chapter 1), unbaked

1 recipe Pecan Streusel (see Chapter 2)

Fresh herbs are a staple of savory cooking, but aromatic herbs can also be used to add flavor to sweet desserts. In this tart, fresh tarragon, which has a mild anise flavor, is paired with ripe peaches and honey. The tarragon lends more than a little sophistication to this gorgeous summer tart.

Preheat the oven to 350°F.

In a large bowl, combine the peaches with the sugar, honey, cornstarch, and tarragon. Let stand for 10 minutes.

Arrange the peaches into the Short Crust and pour any juices over the top. Spread the Pecan Streusel over the top and place the tart pan on a baking sheet.

Bake for 45–55 minutes, or until the fruit is bubbling and the streusel is golden brown. Cool to room temperature before serving.

Chocolate Coconut Caramel Tart

SERVES 8

1 (10") Short Crust for Tarts (see Chapter 1), unbaked

¼ cup milk

¼ cup Salted Caramel Sauce (see Chapter 2), plus more for garnish

3 tablespoons butter, softened

1 tablespoon all-purpose flour

½ cup sugar

1 egg

1 teaspoon vanilla

½ cup sweetened shredded coconut

¼ cup miniature chocolate chips

Toasted coconut for garnish

This tempting tart has a caramel custard base that is studded with bits of chocolate chips and sweet coconut. With a lot of flavor packed in each slice, this decadent dessert is incredibly satisfying. If you want a bit of extra-crunchy chocolate flavor, bake this tart in a chocolate cookie crust.

Preheat the oven to 350°F.

Line the tart with parchment paper or a double layer of aluminum foil and add pie weights or dry beans. Bake for 10 minutes, then remove the paper and weights and bake for an additional 10–12 minutes, or until the crust is lightly golden brown all over. Remove from the oven and set aside to cool. Leave the oven on.

In a medium saucepan over medium heat, bring the milk and Salted Caramel Sauce to a simmer, whisking until the caramel is dissolved. Remove from the heat and cool slightly.

In a large bowl, whisk together the butter, flour, and sugar until well combined.

Add the egg and beat well, then slowly pour in the milk mixture, whisking constantly.

Add the vanilla, then fold in the coconut and chocolate chips.

Pour the mixture into the prepared pastry crust and place on a sheet pan. Bake in the lower third of the oven for 10 minutes, then reduce the heat to 325°F and bake for an additional 25–35 minutes, or until the filling is set at the edges and just slightly wobbly in the center. Cool to room temperature and garnish with the toasted coconut before serving.

Lime Curd and Kiwi Tart

SERVES 8

1 (10") Short Crust for Tarts (see Chapter 1), unbaked

¾ cup sugar

¾ cup lime juice

1 teaspoon lime zest

6 egg yolks

1 tablespoon cornstarch

6 tablespoons unsalted butter

6 kiwis, peeled and sliced thin

½ recipe Stabilized Whipped Cream (see Chapter 2)

Kiwi and lime is a refreshing sweet-tart tropical combination. Not only is this tart delicious, it is easy to make and terribly pretty when it is assembled. From the soothing green colors to the tongue-tickling flavors, this tart makes a lovely end to an al fresco dinner or summer barbecue.

Preheat the oven to 350°F.

Line the tart with parchment paper or a double layer of aluminum foil and add pie weights or dry beans. Bake for 10 minutes, then remove the paper and weights and bake for an additional 10–12 minutes, or until the crust is lightly golden brown all over. Remove from the oven and set aside to cool.

In a medium saucepan, combine the sugar and lime juice and stir until the sugar is melted.

Whisk in the lime zest, egg yolks, and cornstarch. Cook over medium heat, whisking constantly, until bubbling thick, about 10 minutes.

Reduce the heat to low and stir in the butter until melted. Pour the curd through a strainer into the prepared crust. Chill for 4 hours.

Once the tart has chilled, arrange the slices of kiwi on the top in overlapping circles. Pipe the Stabilized Whipped Cream around the edge of the tart. Chill for 30 minutes before serving.

PART 3

Savory Situations

Welcome to the wonderful world of savory pies! Today, you'll find these comfort-food favorites everywhere from brunch menus to fine dining restaurants. And when it comes to savory pies, there is an entire world of cooking techniques and exotic ingredients like goat cheese, chipotle, bacon, wasabi, habanero peppers, black truffles, and more that will take your pie from drab to daring. This new breed of high-end, savory pies featured in this part will delight your taste buds and excite your senses. So leave your old recipes at the door and get involved in some Savory Situations.

❧ Chapter 6 ❧

Dinner Pies

Say goodbye to plain, old, uninspired chicken pot pie and say hello to a new generation of upscale, show-stopping, gourmet creations! In this chapter, you'll find hearty steak pie flavored with black truffle, lobster topped with puff pastry in a creamy sauce, and savory tarts filled with roasted peppers and tangy goat cheese. And these are just a few of the many flavor combinations that are sure to impress. With pies this good, there is no way your dinner will be boring!

Herbed Chicken Pie

SERVES 8

4 tablespoons butter

1 medium onion, finely chopped

1 rib celery, finely chopped

1 green bell pepper, finely chopped

1 pint button mushrooms, sliced

¼ cup fresh parsley leaves, chopped

2 teaspoons fresh thyme, chopped

1 teaspoon fresh sage, chopped

1 teaspoon fresh rosemary, chopped

½ cup all-purpose flour

½ teaspoon cayenne pepper

½ teaspoon salt

½ teaspoon fresh-ground cracked black pepper

1 cup chicken stock

3 cups shredded roast chicken

1 Mealy Pie Crust (see Chapter 1), unbaked

1 egg, beaten

1 Flaky Pie Crust (see Chapter 1), unbaked

Don't let the title of this recipe fool you, this is not grandma's chicken pot pie. For starters, this pie has a thicker filling made without milk or cream. With less liquid in the filling there is more room for tender, juicy chicken. This pie is also made with fresh aromatic herbs for the best possible flavor. Slice for slice, this hearty pie is a sophisticated take on the plain old pot pie.

Preheat the oven to 425°F.

In a large skillet over medium heat, add the butter. Once it foams, add the onion, celery, bell pepper, and mushrooms. Cook, stirring constantly, until the vegetables are softened, about 8 minutes.

Stir in the parsley, thyme, sage, and rosemary and cook until the herbs are wilted and fragrant, about 2 minutes.

Sprinkle the flour over the vegetable mixture and cook until the flour is golden brown, about 6–8 minutes.

Add the cayenne pepper, salt, and pepper, then reduce the heat to low and whisk in the chicken stock. Cook, whisking constantly, until the mixture thickens and just begins to boil.

Turn off the heat and stir in the shredded chicken. Allow to cool slightly.

Spread the chicken filling into the Mealy Pie Crust. Brush the edge of the crust with the beaten egg. Top with the Flaky Pie Crust and trim the dough to 1" of the pan's edge. Tuck edge of the Flaky Pie Crust under the edge of the Mealy Pie Crust. Crimp the dough using your fingers or a fork. Brush the entire top crust with the beaten egg, and cut 4 slits into the crust to allow steam to vent.

Bake for 12 minutes, then reduce the oven to 350°F and bake for 30–40 more minutes, or until the pie is golden brown and bubbling. Let rest 20 minutes before serving.

Apple, Brie, and Bacon Tart

SERVES 8

1 recipe Blitz Puff Pastry
(see Chapter 1)

1 egg, beaten

6 strips thick-cut bacon,
chopped

¼ cup apple butter

6 ounces Brie cheese, cut
into ¼" slices

2 Granny Smith apples,
cored, and sliced ¼" thick

2 tablespoons fresh-grated
Parmesan cheese

This tart may seem unusual, but it's an upscale take on a traditional cheese plate. Often, Brie and other semisoft cheeses are served with slices of crisp Granny Smiths, buttery crackers, and salty cured meats. In this tart, the meat is crisp bacon, the crackers are flaky puff pastry, and along with fresh apple there is a layer of apple butter to provide a sweet finish.

Preheat the oven to 400°F. Line a baking sheet with parchment paper.

Roll the Blitz Puff Pastry out to ½" thick and trim into a 12" square. Place the pastry on the prepared baking sheet. Brush the beaten egg along the edge of the pastry, about a ½" border, and fold the edges of the pastry in, making a ½" lip around the edge of the pastry. Using a fork, dock the center of the pastry. Cover with plastic and chill for 30 minutes.

In a medium skillet over medium heat, cook the bacon until it just begins to brown. Remove from the pan and drain well.

Spread the apple butter over the center of the puff pastry. Arrange the Brie cheese, apples, and bacon over the apple butter and dust the top with Parmesan.

Bake for 30–40 minutes, or until the pastry is golden and the apples are tender. Cool for 5 minutes before serving.

Tomato, Basil, and Mozzarella Tart

SERVES 8

1 Parmesan Pastry Crust
(see Chapter 1) in a 9" tart
pan, unbaked

1 egg, beaten

8 ounces fresh mozzarella,
sliced ¼" thick

4 ripe Roma tomatoes, sliced
¼" thick

8 fresh basil leaves

3 tablespoons extra-virgin
olive oil

½ teaspoon sea salt

½ teaspoon fresh-ground
cracked black pepper

If you enjoy the fresh flavors of a caprese salad, you will love this tart. Its beauty is found in its simplicity. When you are working with vine-ripe tomatoes, fresh-made mozzarella, and vibrant green basil, the only adornment this not-so-humble pie requires is a golden-brown Parmesan pastry crust, a little olive oil, and some fresh-ground cracked black pepper.

Preheat the oven to 350°F.

Line the Parmesan Pastry Crust with parchment paper or a double layer of aluminum foil and add pie weights or dry beans. Bake for 12 minutes, then remove the paper and weights, brush the inside of the part crust lightly with beaten egg, and bake for an additional 12–15 minutes, or until the crust is golden brown all over. Remove from the oven and cool to room temperature.

Layer the sliced cheese alternately with the sliced tomatoes into the bottom of the tart. Tear the basil leaves and sprinkle them over the top of the tart. Drizzle the olive oil over the cheese and tomatoes, then season with salt and pepper. Serve at room temperature.

Goat Cheese and Roasted Red Pepper Tart

SERVES 8

6 ounces goat cheese

2 ounces cream cheese, room temperature

1 clove garlic, finely minced

¼ teaspoon fresh thyme, chopped

¼ teaspoon oregano

½ teaspoon salt

1 cup frozen spinach, thawed and drained

3 roasted red peppers packed in water, drained

1 (12") All-Butter Pie Crust (see Chapter 1), chilled

1 egg, beaten

The fresh goat cheese used in this recipe has a slightly tangy flavor that is enhanced by the addition of the slightly charred flavor of roasted peppers. If you prefer, you can roast your own peppers. Place the peppers on the grill over medium heat and turn every few minutes until they are uniformly charred. Next, place the charred peppers in a covered bowl for ten minutes before rubbing off the blackened skin.

Preheat the oven to 425°F. Line a baking sheet with parchment paper.

In a large bowl, beat together the goat cheese, cream cheese, garlic, thyme, oregano, and salt until smooth. Fold in the spinach then cover and chill until ready to bake.

Slice the roasted peppers into 1" pieces. Set aside.

Place the pastry on the prepared baking sheet. Brush the beaten egg ½" around the edge of the pastry, then fold over to form a border. Spread the cheese mixture into the center of the tart, then arrange the red pepper slices on the top.

Bake for 10 minutes, then reduce the heat to 350°F and bake for an additional 30–40 minutes, or until the pastry is golden brown and the cheese is bubbling and starting to brown. Serve warm.

Onion Tart

SERVES 8

1 recipe Blitz Puff Pastry (see Chapter 1)

3 medium onions, diced

1 cup chicken stock

8 strips bacon, chopped

3 tablespoons heavy cream

½ teaspoon salt

½ teaspoon fresh-ground cracked pepper

This Onion Tart is simple but elegant. The tender onions and smoky bacon found in this recipe make this dish delicious for brunch, lunch, or dinner. If you can find sweet Vidalia onions in the market, try using them in this recipe; they are milder than white or yellow onions and have a subtle bite.

Preheat the oven to 350°F.

Roll out the Blitz Puff Pastry to an ⅛" thick 12" circle, turning the dough often to make sure it does not stick. Dust the surface with additional flour, if needed.

Fold the dough in half and place it into a 10" tart pan. Unfold and carefully push the dough into the pan, making sure not to pull or stretch the dough. Press the dough against the edge of the tart pan to trim. Use a fork and dock the bottom and sides of the dough well. Cover with plastic and place in the refrigerator to chill.

Heat a medium skillet over medium-high heat. Add the onions and chicken stock and cook until the onions are soft and the liquid has reduced, about 30 minutes. Drain off any excess liquid, then transfer the onions to a bowl and allow to cool.

In the same skillet, over medium heat, cook the bacon until crisp and the fat has rendered. Drain the excess fat.

Combine the cooked bacon with the onions. Stir in the cream and add the salt and pepper.

Pour the mixture into the crust and place the tart pan on a baking sheet. Bake in the lower third of the oven for 30–40 minutes, or until golden brown and the crust is set. Cool slightly before serving.

Sharp Cheddar and Mushroom Tart

SERVES 8

1 Parmesan Pastry Crust
(see Chapter 1)

¼ ounce dry wild
mushrooms

½ cup boiling water

2 tablespoons butter

1 medium onion, diced

1 pound button mushrooms,
sliced

2 cloves garlic, minced

2 tablespoons all-purpose
flour

2 tablespoons lemon juice

2 egg yolks

½ teaspoon salt

¼ teaspoon fresh-ground
cracked black pepper

½ teaspoon smoked paprika

4 ounces extra-sharp Cheddar cheese, shredded

When the intense, robust, hearty flavor profile of the dry wild mushrooms is merged with the sharp, clean taste of Cheddar cheese, the result is this beautiful pie that will have your guests going back for seconds. Once the dry mushrooms are reconstituted in hot water, you have not only the mushrooms but a mushroom broth that adds another layer of rich flavor.

Preheat the oven to 350°F.

Line the Parmesan Pastry Crust with parchment paper or a double layer of aluminum foil and add pie weights or dry beans. Bake for 12 minutes, then remove the paper and weights and bake for an additional 10–15 minutes, or until the crust is golden brown all over. Remove from the oven and set aside to cool. Leave the oven on.

Combine the dry mushrooms with the water. Let stand for 10 minutes, or until rehydrated. Drain the mushrooms, reserving the liquid, and chop well.

In a large skillet over medium heat, add the butter. Once the butter begins to foam, add the onions and cook until softened, about 5 minutes. Add the sliced mushrooms and cook until tender, about 5 minutes. Add the garlic and rehydrated mushrooms and cook until fragrant, about 30 seconds. Add the flour to the mushrooms and cook for 1 minute.

Stir in ½ cup of the reserved mushroom liquid with the lemon juice and cook, stirring constantly, until thickened, about 5 minutes. Reduce the heat to low.

Whisk together ¼ cup of the reserved mushroom liquid with the egg yolks. Whisk the mixture into the mushrooms. Increase the heat to medium and cook until the liquid coats the back of a spoon, about 3 minutes. Stir in the salt, pepper, and paprika.

Pour the mushroom mixture into the prepared pastry crust, then spread the Cheddar over the top.

Bake for 12–15 minutes, or until the cheese is melted and starting to bubble. Cool for 10 minutes before serving.

Apple and Brie Tart with Bacon Crumble

SERVES 8

1 (10") Parmesan Pastry Crust (see Chapter 1)

1 tablespoon whole-grain mustard

8 ounces Brie cheese, sliced into ¼" thick slices

1 Fuji apple, cored and thinly sliced

3 strips thick-cut bacon, cooked crisp

⅓ cup all-purpose flour

⅓ cup packed light brown sugar

3 tablespoons butter, cubed and chilled

2 tablespoons honey

Want to impress with something completely unexpected yet wholly delicious? The unique topping on this not-so-humble pie features finely ground bacon, which gives this sweet tart a salty, savory finish. The flavors in this tart are similar to those found on a traditional cheese platter, only better! Serve this as a main dish at brunch or with a crisp salad for dinner.

Preheat the oven to 350°F.

Line the Parmesan Pastry Crust with parchment paper or a double layer of aluminum foil and add pie weights or dry beans. Bake for 12 minutes, then remove the paper and weights, brush the inside of the part crust lightly with beaten egg, and bake for an additional 12–15 minutes, or until the crust is golden brown all over. Remove from the oven and cool to room temperature. Increase the oven to 400°F.

With a pastry brush, spread the mustard into the pastry crust. Layer the Brie evenly in the bottom of the crust, then layer the apples over the top.

In a food processor or blender, place the bacon strips and process until very finely ground.

Combine the ground bacon with the flour and sugar and mix well. Using your fingers, rub in the butter until the mixture resembles coarse sand.

Heat the broiler. Spread the crumble evenly over the top of the tart. Broil about 5" from the heating element for 2–3 minutes, or until the bacon is crisp and brown and the cheese has begun to melt. Remove the tart from the oven and cool for 5 minutes before drizzling the honey over the top. Serve immediately.

Sun-dried Tomato, Pesto, and Mozzarella Tart

SERVES 8

1 (12") Parmesan Pastry Crust (see Chapter 1), chilled

1 egg, beaten

4 ounces fresh mozzarella, sliced ¼" thick

½ cup sun-dried tomatoes, thinly sliced

¼ cup fresh-grated Parmesan cheese

¼ cup prepared pesto sauce

¼ teaspoon salt

¼ teaspoon fresh-ground cracked pepper

Sun-dried tomatoes have a sweet yet tangy flavor and a pretty deep-red color that makes this tart particularly eye catching when it is fresh from the oven. The bubbling, golden-brown cheese is strewn with bits of sundried tomato and pesto for a look and flavor that is distinctively Italian—and thoroughly high class.

Preheat the oven to 425°F. Line a baking sheet with parchment paper.

Place the pastry on the prepared baking sheet. Brush the beaten egg ½" around the edge of the pastry then fold over to form a border. Cover and chill for 30 minutes.

Arrange the mozzarella slices over the pastry. Place the sun-dried tomato strips and Parmesan cheese over the mozzarella. Drizzle the pesto over the top, then season with the salt and pepper.

Bake for 10 minutes, then reduce the heat to 350°F and bake for an additional 30–40 minutes, or until the pastry is golden brown and the cheese is bubbling and starting to brown. Serve warm.

Butternut Squash and Kale Pie

SERVES 8

1 (9") Pepper Jack Pastry Crust (see Chapter 1), unbaked

1 tablespoon olive oil

1 medium butternut squash, peeled and chopped (about 3 cups)

1 tablespoon butter

1 medium onion, diced

2 cloves garlic, minced

½ teaspoon smoked paprika

½ teaspoon salt

¼ teaspoon thyme

¼ teaspoon crushed red pepper flakes

1 pound kale leaves, roughly chopped

¼ cup water

¼ cup shredded Parmesan cheese

The slightly bitter flavor of the green, leafy kale found in this gorgeous pie is balanced by the sweet flavor of roasted butternut squash. Aside from tasting amazing, this layered pie is also beautiful on the plate; its alternating layers of dusky orange and green are a welcome addition to any fall or winter feast!

Preheat the oven to 375°F. Line the pie crust with parchment paper or a double layer of aluminum foil and add pie weights or dry beans. Bake for 10–12 minutes, then remove the paper and weights and bake for an additional 10–12 minutes, or until the crust is golden brown all over. Remove from the oven and set aside to cool. Increase the oven temperature to 450°F.

In a large bowl, combine the oil and butternut squash. Toss to coat, then spread the squash in an even layer on a parchment-lined baking sheet. Roast for 1 hour, or until very tender and caramelized. Remove from the oven to cool to room temperature. Reduce the oven temperature to 350°F.

In a large skillet, melt the butter over medium heat. Once it foams, add the onion and cook until tender, about 5 minutes. Add the garlic, paprika, salt, thyme, and crushed red pepper and cook for 1 minute, or until fragrant.

Add the kale and water and stir to coat the kale. Cook until the kale is tender and wilted, about 6–8 minutes. Once wilted, remove the pan from the heat and allow to cool to room temperature.

To assemble the pie, spread half the roasted squash on the bottom of the pastry crust. Next, add the kale mixture and then top with the remaining squash. Sprinkle the cheese evenly over the top.

Bake for 30–35 minutes, or until the filling is hot and the cheese is melted. Cool for 10 minutes before serving.

Herb, Fennel, and Cheese Pie

SERVES 8

1 (9") All-Butter Pie Crust (see Chapter 1), unbaked

3 tablespoons butter

1 medium fennel bulb, chopped

1 medium onion, finely chopped

½ teaspoon salt

2 cups ricotta cheese

1 cup crumbled feta cheese

3 eggs, beaten

2 tablespoons all-purpose flour

¼ cup chopped fresh dill

¼ teaspoon black pepper

Fresh dill, tangy cheese, and sweet fennel combine to create a surprisingly powerful filling for this decadent pie. The flavor of fennel is similar to that of anise seed, but when it is cooked the flavor mellows and becomes slightly sweet. This sweetness helps to temper the tang of the salty, fresh feta cheese.

Preheat the oven to 375°F. Line the pie crust with parchment paper or a double layer of aluminum foil and add pie weights or dry beans. Bake for 10–12 minutes, then remove the paper and weights and bake for an additional 10–12 minutes, or until the crust is golden brown all over. Remove from the oven and set aside to cool. Leave the oven on.

In a medium skillet over medium heat, add the butter. Once it foams, add the chopped fennel, onions, and salt. Cook, stirring frequently, until tender, about 10 minutes.

Transfer to a large bowl and stir in ricotta, feta, eggs, flour, dill, and pepper. Stir until the mixture is well combined.

Spread the cheese mixture into the pastry crust. Bake for 30–40 minutes, or until the filling is set and starting to brown lightly on the top. Cool for 20 minutes at room temperature before serving.

New England Clam and Potato Pie

SERVES 8

3 medium russet potatoes, peeled and cut into 1" pieces

2 cups clam juice

6 strips thick-cut bacon, roughly chopped

1 medium onion, peeled and finely chopped

1 carrot, peeled and finely chopped

1 rib celery, finely chopped

1 bay leaf

1 clove garlic, minced

1 teaspoon thyme

¼ teaspoon cayenne pepper

2 tablespoons flour

3 cups shucked clams, roughly chopped

¼ teaspoon salt

¼ teaspoon freshly ground cracked black pepper

1 (9") Mealy Pie Crust (see Chapter 1)

3 tablespoons chilled butter, cut into small pieces

1 egg, beaten

1 recipe All-Butter Pie Crust (see Chapter 1)

Clam and potato chowder is a classic comfort-food dish. In fact, the only thing that can make a bowl of chowder more comforting is to bake it in a buttery pastry crust. This upscale pie is filling, loaded with clams and tender potatoes, and is a fun twist on a plain bowl of soup. Serve this up in the fall and winter to ward off the cold with style and sophistication.

In a large pot over medium-high heat, add the potatoes and clam juice. Boil until fork tender, about 10–15 minutes. Drain well, then return to the pot and lightly mash with a fork. Set aside.

In a medium skillet over medium-low heat, add the bacon and cook until very crisp, about 8–10 minutes. Transfer bacon to a paper towel–lined plate to drain.

Add onions, carrots, celery, and bay leaf to the rendered bacon fat and cook until the vegetables are softened and just starting to color, about 15–18 minutes.

Add the garlic, thyme, and cayenne pepper and cook for 1 minute, or until fragrant. Remove from the heat to cool slightly and remove the bay leaf.

In a large bowl, combine the potatoes, bacon mixture, flour, clams, salt, and pepper. Mix until well combined.

Preheat oven to 400°F.

Spread the clam filling into the Mealy Pie Crust and dot the top with the butter. Brush the edge with the beaten egg, then top with the All-Butter Pie Crust and trim the dough to within 1" of the pan's edge. Tuck the edge of the All-Butter Pie Crust under the edge of the Mealy Pie Crust. Crimp the dough using your fingers or a fork. Brush the entire top crust with the beaten egg and cut a little hole in the center of the pie to allow steam to vent.

Bake for 50–55 minutes, or until golden brown. Allow to rest for 20 minutes before serving.

Seared Ahi Tuna and Wasabi Crème Tartlets

SERVES

2 recipes All-Butter Pie Crust (see Chapter 1)

1 tablespoon toasted sesame oil

2 tablespoons soy sauce

1 tablespoon minced pickled ginger, plus more for garnish

1 clove garlic, minced

1 green onion thinly sliced, plus more for garnish

1 teaspoon lime juice

2 (8-ounce) ahi tuna steaks, 1" thick

2 tablespoons prepared wasabi

½ cup sour cream

Ahi tuna is a sushi bar favorite—and for good reason. It has a clean, meaty flavor, it is easy to prepare, and it dazzles diners with its beautiful ruby-red coloring. In this tart, slices of perfectly seared ahi tuna are drizzled with a tangy wasabi crème and served in a buttery tart shell.

Preheat the oven to 400°F. Line a baking sheet with parchment paper.

Roll the All-Butter Pie Crust out to ¼" thick and trim to fit into 8 (4") tart pans. Place the pastry into the pans, making sure not to stretch the dough, and dock with a fork. Line the tart with parchment paper or a double layer of aluminum foil and add pie weights or dry beans. Bake for 12 minutes, then remove the paper and weights and bake for an additional 10–15 minutes, or until the crusts are golden brown all over. Remove from the oven and set aside to cool.

In a large freezer bag, combine the sesame oil, soy sauce, pickled ginger, garlic, green onion, and lime juice. Add the tuna steaks and turn to coat. Close the bag, pressing out the air, and refrigerate for 1 hour.

In a small bowl, whisk together the wasabi and sour cream until smooth. Cover and refrigerate until ready to serve.

Heat a nonstick skillet over medium-high to high heat. When the pan is hot, spray lightly with nonstick cooking spray. Remove the tuna steaks from the marinade and sear them for 1–2 minutes per side, depending on your preferred level of doneness. Remove from pan and slice into ¼" thick slices.

Arrange the sliced tuna in the prepared tart shells. Drizzle with the wasabi cream and garnish with green onions and pickled ginger. Serve immediately.

Smoked Salmon and Dill Tartlets

SERVES 8

2 recipes Parmesan Pastry Crust (see Chapter 1)

½ cup cream cheese

½ cup sour cream

½ teaspoon salt

½ teaspoon fresh-ground cracked black pepper

1 teaspoon lemon zest

2 tablespoons fresh dill, chopped

16 ounces cold smoked salmon

Fresh lemon juice, for garnish

With its mild smoky flavor and a gorgeous fiery-orange color, smoked salmon is a true delicacy. This tart uses cold smoked salmon, which has a delicate flavor and texture that blends well with the creamy mixture of cream cheese, sour cream, fresh dill, and lemon juice that works as the pie's base. These tarts make a lovely light meal or a hearty appetizer.

Preheat the oven to 350°F.

Roll out the Parmesan Pastry Crust until it is ⅛" thick. Cut the pastry into 8 pieces. Line 8 (4") tart pans with the dough, pressing the dough against the rim of the pan to trim. Line the pastry with parchment paper or a double layer of aluminum foil and add pie weights or dry beans. Bake for 8–10 minutes, then remove the paper and weights and bake for an additional 10–12 minutes, or until the tart shells are golden brown all over.

In a medium bowl, cream together the cream cheese, sour cream, salt, pepper, lemon zest, and dill. Beat until smooth and well combined. Divide the dill mixture evenly between the pastry crusts and spread to form an even layer.

Cut the smoked salmon into 1" pieces, then divide evenly between the tarts in an even layer. Squeeze fresh lemon juice over each tart to garnish. Serve cold or at room temperature.

Mushroom and Goat Cheese Tart

SERVES 8

1 Parmesan Pastry Crust (see Chapter 1), unbaked

2 tablespoons butter

1 medium onion, diced

1 pound button mushrooms, cut into ½" pieces

½ teaspoon salt

2 cloves garlic, minced

2 tablespoons all-purpose flour

¼ cup chicken or vegetable stock

1 tablespoon heavy cream

¼ teaspoon thyme

4 ounces soft goat cheese

This tart is topped with what the French call a *duxelles*, a mixture of mushrooms and either onions or shallots that is cooked in butter until soft. This recipe uses this typical stuffing as the filling for this tasty tart. Under the duxelles, there is a layer of goat cheese that melts slightly under the warm mushroom mixture, making this dish even more creamy and irresistible.

Preheat the oven to 425°F.

Line the Parmesan Pastry Crust with parchment paper or a double layer of aluminum foil and add pie weights or dry beans. Bake for 12 minutes, then remove the paper and weights and bake for an additional 12–15 minutes, or until the crust is golden brown. Remove from the oven and set aside to cool.

In a large skillet over medium heat, add the butter. Once the butter begins to foam, add the onions and cook until softened, about 5 minutes.

Add the sliced mushrooms and salt and cook until tender, about 5 minutes.

Add the garlic and cook until fragrant, about 30 seconds.

Add the flour to the mushrooms and cook for 1 minute. Stir in the stock, heavy cream, and thyme and cook, stirring constantly, until thickened, about 5 minutes.

Carefully spread the goat cheese into the bottom of the prepared crust. Spoon the mushroom mixture evenly over the top while still hot. Serve immediately.

Caramelized Onion, Potato, and Pancetta Tart

SERVES 8

1 medium red onion, thinly sliced

1 teaspoon sugar

1 russet potato, peeled and thinly sliced

4 ounces pancetta, chopped

1 Parmesan Pastry Crust (see Chapter 1)

1 cup shredded Gruyère cheese

1 egg

½ cup heavy cream

⅛ teaspoon fresh-grated nutmeg

¼ teaspoon salt

½ teaspoon fresh-ground black pepper

It is easy to imagine a slice of this tart served at a bustling sidewalk bistro. The star of this tart is pancetta, the Italian form of bacon which is cured but not smoked. Pancetta has a cleaner pork flavor and does not overpower the other flavors. In this dish, the pancetta is combined with tender potatoes, sweet caramelized onions, and creamy Gruyère cheese to create a layered tart that has as much visual appeal as it has delicious flavor.

In a heavy skillet heat olive oil over medium-low heat, then add the sliced onions and sugar. Cook for 45 minutes to 1 hour, or until the onions are deeply golden brown. Stir the onions often to prevent burning, and add a little water if the pan becomes dry or the onions start to stick. Once caramelized, remove the pan from the heat and cool the mixture completely to room temperature.

In a medium pot, add the sliced potatoes and enough water to just cover the slices. Bring the mixture to a boil and cook until the potatoes are just tender, about 5 minutes. Drain the potatoes well.

In a small skillet over medium heat, add the pancetta. Cook it until it is very crisp, about 6–8 minutes. Transfer the pancetta to a paper towel–lined plate to drain.

Preheat the oven to 375°F.

To assemble the tart, begin by spreading ½ the caramelized onions on the bottom of the pastry. Next, sprinkle ½ the pancetta, ⅓ of the Gruyère, and top with ½ the potato slices. Repeat this process, then top the tart with the remaining Gruyère.

In a small bowl, beat together the egg, cream, nutmeg, salt, and pepper. Pour this over the filling.

Bake for 40–50 minutes, or until the filling is just set in the center and the top is golden brown. Cool for 10 minutes before serving.

Polenta Pie with Italian Sausage and Roasted Peppers

SERVES 8

1 tablespoon olive oil

1 medium onion, finely diced

2 cloves garlic, minced

3 cups low-sodium chicken or vegetable broth

8 tablespoons butter

1½ cups quick-cooking polenta

6 ounces fresh bulk Italian sausage

1 (14-ounce) can fire-roasted crushed tomatoes, drained

½ teaspoon ground fennel

½ teaspoon oregano

¼ teaspoon crushed red pepper

6 ounces fresh mozzarella, cut into ¼" thick slices

¼ cup shredded Parmesan cheese

Polenta is an incredibly versatile dish. It can be cooked soft, where it has a creamy texture like southern grits, or it can be cooked firm and either baked or grilled. In this savory dish, the polenta serves as the crust for a filling made of spicy Italian sausage, fire-roasted tomatoes, and mozzarella cheese that makes this pie more than posh.

In a medium pot over medium heat, add the olive oil. Once it ripples and shimmers, add the onions and cook until they soften, about 5 minutes.

Add the garlic and cook until fragrant, about 30 seconds.

Add the broth and 3 tablespoons of the butter and bring the mixture to a simmer. Slowly whisk in the polenta and cook until very thick, about 5 minutes.

Pour the polenta into a shallow dish that has been sprayed with non-stick cooking spray. Refrigerate, covered, for 30 minutes, or up to 2 days.

In a medium skillet over medium heat, add the remaining butter. Once it starts to foam, add the Italian sausage and cook, stirring constantly, until the sausage is browned.

Add the crushed tomatoes, fennel, oregano, and crushed red pepper. Cook until the mixture comes to a simmer. Remove the pan from the heat and allow to cool slightly.

Preheat the oven to 375°F.

Slice the polenta into ¼" thick slices and line a 9" pie plate with ½ of the slices, overlapping them slightly so the bottom of the plate is completely covered. Spread the Italian sausage mixture over the polenta, top with the mozzarella slices, then cover with the remaining slices of polenta. Sprinkle the Parmesan cheese over the top.

Bake for 20–30 minutes, or until the filling is bubbling and the cheese on top has browned. Cool for 10 minutes before serving.

Spinach and Artichoke Tart

SERVES 8

1 Parmesan Pastry Crust, unbaked (see Chapter 1)

2 tablespoons butter

½ medium onion, finely chopped

1 clove garlic, minced

½ teaspoon oregano

¼ teaspoon ground fennel

¼ teaspoon crushed red pepper

¼ teaspoon salt

4 ounces cream cheese, softened

5 ounces frozen artichoke hearts, thawed and chopped

5 ounces frozen chopped spinach, thawed and squeezed dry

1 cup mozzarella, shredded

½ cup smoked provolone, shredded

¼ cup Parmesan, shredded

Spinach and artichoke are a popular dip combination; after all, who can resist the nutty flavor of artichokes when mixed with mild spinach in a bubbling hot cheese sauce? Now that same enticing flavor combination makes a guest appearance at your dinner table. If you like, you can turn this tart into bite-sized servings for a cocktail party. Just prepare the tarts in a mini muffin tin rather than a larger tart pan.

Preheat the oven to 425°F.

Line the Parmesan Pastry Crust with parchment paper or a double layer of aluminum foil and add pie weights or dry beans. Bake for 12 minutes, then remove the paper and weights and bake for an additional 12–15 minutes, or until the crust is golden brown. Remove from the oven and set aside to cool. Leave the oven on.

In a medium skillet over medium heat, add the butter. Once it foams, add the onion and cook until just softened, about 3 minutes.

Add the garlic, oregano, fennel, crushed red pepper, and salt and cook until fragrant, about 1 minute. Remove the pan from the heat and allow to cool.

In a large bowl, combine the cream cheese, artichokes, spinach, mozzarella, provolone, and Parmesan cheese. Mix well, then stir in the onion mixture.

Spread the spinach mixture into the prepared crust. Bake for 10–15 minutes, or until the filling is hot and just starting to bubble. Cool for 10 minutes before serving.

Shredded Beef Hand Pies with Spiced Cheese Sauce

SERVES 8

2 teaspoons vegetable oil

2 pounds bone-in beef short ribs

1 tablespoon kosher salt

2 teaspoons fresh-ground cracked black pepper

4 strips thick-cut smoked bacon, cut in ½

1 medium onion, peeled and quartered

4 cloves garlic, crushed

½ cup diced tomatoes

½ cup fresh cilantro

1 bay leaf

1 cinnamon stick

1 tablespoon cumin

1 tablespoon smoked paprika

1 tablespoon chili powder

2 teaspoons coriander

2 teaspoons kosher salt

2 cups beef stock

1½ cups pepper jack cheese, shredded

2 recipes Flaky Pie Crust (see Chapter 1), not pressed into pie pans

1 egg, beaten

2 tablespoons butter

¼ onion, minced

½ jalapeño, finely diced

¼ teaspoon smoked paprika

3 tablespoons all-purpose flour

¾ cup whole milk

½ teaspoon salt

Slow-cooked short ribs produce a tender, buttery meat that is traditionally a perfect addition to pasta or salad dishes. This recipe takes a backyard favorite and bakes it into a delectable little pie. Here, short ribs are slow cooked with Latin spices and shredded, and on the side there is a spicy pepper jack cheese sauce for your dipping pleasure.

In a medium skillet over medium-high heat, add the oil. While the oil heats, season all sides of the ribs with salt and pepper.

Once the oil ripples and shimmers in the pan, add the ribs and cook until darkly browned on all sides, about 3–5 minutes per side.

While the ribs brown, in a slow cooker, add the bacon, onion, garlic, tomato, cilantro, bay leaf, cinnamon, cumin, paprika, chili powder, coriander, and salt.

Top with the ribs and add enough beef stock to just cover the ribs. Add water, if needed. Cook on low for 8 hours, then turn off the slow cooker and cool for 1 hour in the liquid before transferring to a container to cool completely. Once cool, shred the meat and mix with 1 cup of the pepper jack cheese.

Preheat the oven to 425°F. Line a baking sheet with parchment paper.

Cut the pastry into 16 (4") rounds or squares. Place a heaping tablespoon of the filling into the pastry, then brush the edges of the pastry with beaten egg. Place a second piece of dough over the top and pinch or crimp the edges with a fork to seal. Place the pies on the prepared baking sheet and chill for 1 hour.

Brush the tops of the pies with beaten egg, then cut a tiny slit into the top of each pie to vent steam. Bake for 10 minutes, then reduce the heat to 350°F and bake for 20–25 minutes more, or until the pastry is golden brown all over. Remove from the oven and allow to cool while you prepare the cheese sauce.

In a medium saucepan over medium heat, add the butter. Once it foams, add the onion, jalapeño, and paprika. Cook until the onion and jalapeño are softened, about 2 minutes.

Sprinkle the flour over the butter mixture and cook for 2–3 minutes, or until the flour is just starting to turn a light golden color. Reduce the heat to low and slowly whisk in the milk. Once all the milk is added, increase the heat to medium again and whisk until the mixture comes to a boil and thickens, about 8 minutes. Season with the salt.

Turn off the heat and add the remainder of the pepper jack cheese. Stir until thoroughly melted.

Serve the pies while they are still warm with the sauce drizzled over the top.

Creamy Prosciutto and Leek Pie

SERVES 8

4 ounces prosciutto, chopped

2 tablespoons butter

2 leeks, white part only, cleaned and chopped

1 (9") Parmesan Pastry Crust (see Chapter 1), unbaked

2 eggs

3 ounces cream cheese

1 cup cream, room temperature

Pinch fresh-grated nutmeg

½ teaspoon salt

½ teaspoon fresh-ground cracked pepper

1 cup Gruyère cheese, grated

Prosciutto, an Italian dry-cured ham, has a delicate and slightly salty flavor, which is similar to bacon but without the smoke. Leeks, a cousin of the onion, also have a delicate, mild flavor. The prosciutto and leeks give this tart a delicate and refined flavor that complements the subtle nuttiness of the Gruyère cheese. Warm slices of this pie make an elegant addition to any meal.

In a medium skillet over medium heat, add the chopped prosciutto. Sauté, stirring often, until crisp, about 8–10 minutes.

Transfer the prosciutto to a paper towel–lined plate to drain. Using the same pan, melt the butter until it foams. Add the leeks and sauté until softened, about 5 minutes. Remove from the heat and allow to cool.

Preheat the oven to 375°F. Line the pie crust with parchment paper or a double layer of aluminum foil and add pie weights or dry beans. Bake for 12 minutes, then remove the paper and weights and bake for an additional 10 minutes, or until the crust is golden brown all over. Remove from the oven and set aside to cool.

In a medium bowl, whisk together the eggs and cream cheese until smooth.

Stir in the cream, nutmeg, salt, and pepper and whisk until well combined.

Spread the leeks, prosciutto, and Gruyère evenly on the bottom of the crust. Carefully pour the egg mixture over the top.

Bake for 30–40 minutes, or until the filling is set and starting to brown lightly on the top. Cool for 20 minutes before serving.

Steak and Black Truffle Pie

SERVES 8

2 pounds chuck roast, cut into 1" cubes

1 teaspoon black truffle salt

1 teaspoon fresh-ground cracked pepper

½ cup all-purpose flour

4 tablespoons vegetable oil, divided

3 cups beef stock

1 cup water

2 carrots, peeled and cut into ½" pieces

4 tablespoons butter

1 medium onion, diced

2 cloves garlic, minced

1 teaspoon fresh thyme, chopped

⅓ cup all-purpose flour

2 tablespoons black truffle butter

1 Flaky Pie Crust (see Chapter 1), rolled out to 12" × 15"

Black truffles are renowned the world over for their superior flavor and aroma. However, they are very expensive and are not always available fresh, even in gourmet markets. In this pie, the flavor of black truffles comes from black truffle salt and black truffle butter. Both have the same earthy flavor as actual black truffles, but are readily available in most gourmet stores—and they are much more affordable.

In a large bowl, combine the chuck roast, truffle salt, pepper, and flour until all the meat is evenly coated. In a large pot, heat 2 tablespoons of the vegetable oil over medium-high heat until it ripples and shimmers. Add ½ of the beef to the pot and brown well on all sides. Remove from the pot and add the remaining vegetable oil. Brown the remaining meat, then add the first addition of meat back to the pot.

Add the beef stock and water to the pot and bring the mixture to a boil. Reduce the heat to medium-low and cook the meat, covered, for 40 minutes. Add the carrots and cook for 10 minutes, or until the carrots are tender. Strain the meat and vegetables from the cooking liquid to cool. Reserve the cooking liquid.

In a large skillet over medium heat, melt the butter until it foams. Add the onion and cook until tender, about 10 minutes. Add the garlic and thyme. Cook until fragrant, about 1 minute. Sprinkle the flour over the top of the mixture and cook until no raw flour remains.

Add 1 cup of the reserved cooking liquid to the onion mixture and cook, stirring constantly, until thick and smooth, about 5 minutes. Remove from the heat and add in the steak and vegetables.

Preheat the oven to 425°F. Pour the meat mixture into a 2½-quart casserole dish. Dot the top of the meat mixture with the truffle butter, then cover with the Flaky Pie Crust, tucking the edges of the pastry into the pan, and cut 2 or 3 slits into the pastry to vent steam.

Bake for 20 minutes, then reduce the heat to 350°F and bake for an additional 30–40 minutes, or until the pastry is golden brown and the filling is bubbling. Cool for 30 minutes before serving.

Lobster Pie

SERVES 8

2 strips bacon, chopped

4 tablespoons butter

1 medium russet potato, peeled and cut into ½" pieces

1 medium onion, diced

½ medium green bell pepper, diced

2 cloves garlic, minced

½ teaspoon thyme

½ teaspoon smoked paprika

½ teaspoon salt

½ teaspoon fresh-ground cracked black pepper

⅓ cup all-purpose flour

3 cups half-and-half

1 pound peeled, deveined shrimp

1 pound fresh lobster tail, shelled and cut into ½" pieces

1 egg, beaten

1 recipe Blitz Puff Pastry (see Chapter 1), rolled out to 12" × 15"

With its rich, sweet, buttery flavor and silky texture, lobster is a luxurious ingredient. The lobster in this pie is cooked in a velvety cream sauce and topped with a puff pastry crust to add an extra sumptuous finish. If you cannot find fresh lobster, feel free to substitute lump crab meat.

Preheat the oven to 375°F.

In a medium saucepan, cook the chopped bacon over medium heat until crisp. Drain the bacon on paper towels, leaving the fat.

Return the pan to the heat and add the butter. Once the butter foams, add the potatoes, onions, and bell peppers. Cook, stirring constantly, until the potatoes become tender, about 10 minutes.

Add the garlic, thyme, paprika, salt, and pepper and cook until fragrant, about 1 minute.

Sprinkle the flour over the vegetable mixture and cook until no raw flour remains. Slowly stir in the half-and-half and bring the mixture to a simmer, stirring constantly, until it starts to thicken, about 8 minutes.

Once it thickens, stir in the shrimp and lobster. Cook for 1 minute, then remove the pan from the heat and stir in the bacon.

Pour the seafood filling into a 2½-quart baking dish and brush the edge of the pan with the beaten egg. Top with the Blitz Puff Pastry, pressing the pastry against the edge of the pan until it adheres. Trim the pastry so it hangs ½" over the edge of the dish. Brush the pastry with the egg and cut a few small vents in the center of the pastry to allow steam to vent.

Bake for 30–40 minutes, or until the pastry is brown and the filling is bubbling. Cool for 30 minutes before serving.

Caramelized Onion and Gruyère Tart

SERVES 8

3 strips thick-cut bacon, chopped

3 large or 4 medium yellow onions, peeled and sliced ¼" thick

2 teaspoons sugar

½ cup water

3 cloves garlic, minced

1 teaspoon apple cider vinegar

¼ teaspoon fresh-grated nutmeg

1 teaspoon hot sauce

1 recipe Blitz Puff Pastry (see Chapter 1)

1 egg, beaten

1 cup Gruyère cheese, shredded

¼ teaspoon smoked paprika

Caramelized onions are a magical ingredient. They add complex flavors, depth, and sweetness to any dish to which they are added. In this sophisticated tart, the caramelized onions really stand out, and are complemented by nutty Gruyère cheese and buttery puff pastry. Slices of this tart are a lovely accompaniment to a rich cup of soup.

In a large sauté pan over medium heat, cook the bacon until crisp. Remove the bacon from the pan and allow to drain. Do not drain off the fat.

Add the onions to the pan along with the sugar and cook for 1 minute, then reduce the heat to medium-low and add ¼ cup of the water.

Cook, stirring constantly, until the onions are well caramelized, about 30 minutes. If the pan becomes too dry or the onions begin to stick, add the additional water. Add the garlic, apple cider vinegar, nutmeg, and hot sauce. Cook until the garlic is fragrant and the vinegar has reduced, about 5 minutes. Remove from the heat and allow to cool.

Preheat the oven to 425°F. Line a baking sheet with parchment paper.

Roll out the Blitz Puff Pastry to ⅛" thick, then use a pizza wheel to cut out a 12" circle. Place on the prepared baking sheet and brush the edge of the pastry with beaten egg, about a ½" border. Fold the pastry in, forming a ½" rim. Dock the center of the pastry, cover with plastic, and chill for 30 minutes.

Once chilled, spread the caramelized onions over the pastry. Top with the cooked bacon and the Gruyère, and dust the top with the paprika.

Bake for 15 minutes, then reduce the heat to 350°F and bake for an additional 30–40 minutes, or until the pastry is crisp and golden. Serve warm.

Individual Eggs Benedict Tarts

SERVES 8

1 recipe All-Butter Pie Crust (see Chapter 1), unbaked

8 slices Canadian bacon

3 egg yolks

¼ teaspoon Dijon mustard

1 tablespoon lemon juice

1 dash hot pepper sauce

½ cup butter

1 teaspoon white vinegar

8 eggs

4 tablespoons fresh chives, chopped

There is something about eggs Benedict that is utterly irresistible. The combination of grilled ham, a perfectly poached egg, and lemony hollandaise sauce is always a crowd pleaser. In this recipe, the traditional plain English muffin is replaced with a crisp round of buttery pastry and topped with freshly snipped chives for an elegant finish.

Preheat the oven to 375°F. Cut the pastry crusts into 8 (4") rounds. Flute the edges with your fingers, then place on a parchment-lined baking sheet. Dock the center of the pastry rounds with a fork. Bake for 10–12 minutes, or until golden brown all over and crisp. Set aside to cool and reduce the oven temperature to 200°F.

Spray an oven-proof skillet with nonstick cooking spray. Heat the pan over medium heat. Once hot, add the Canadian bacon and cook until they are browned on both sides, about 2 minutes per side. Place the pan in a warm oven until ready to use.

In the work bowl of a blender, add the egg yolks, mustard, lemon juice, and hot pepper sauce and blend for 1 minute. Melt the butter in the microwave until it is hot and steamy, about 1½ minutes. With the blender running on high speed, slowly drizzle in the butter. Once combined, wrap the blender work bowl in foil and set aside.

Bring a large saucepan filled ¾ of the way full with water to a simmer. Once the water simmers, add in the vinegar.

Crack the eggs into a small bowl. Place the bowl close to the surface of the water and gently drop the egg into the water. With a spoon, gently nudge the egg whites closer to their yolks. Repeat with as many eggs as will fit in the pan without crowding.

Cook for 3–4 minutes, depending on your preferred level of doneness. Lift the cooked eggs out of the water with a slotted spoon.

To assemble, place one Canadian bacon slice on a pastry round. Top with the poached egg. Spoon hollandaise sauce over and garnish with fresh chives. Serve immediately.

Roasted Heirloom Tomato Tart

SERVES 8

1 recipe Blitz Puff Pastry (see Chapter 1), rolled out to 12" × 15"

2 pounds heirloom tomatoes, quartered

3 tablespoons extra-virgin olive oil

2 teaspoons fresh thyme, chopped

1 teaspoon fresh rosemary, chopped

½ teaspoon salt

½ teaspoon fresh-ground cracked black pepper

½ cup grated Romano cheese

Heirloom tomatoes come in many varieties, colors, and flavors. It is best to use the tomatoes you prefer, but for this tart a variety of colors makes for a pretty presentation—and a more mouthwatering experience. As a final touch, you may want to drizzle a little good-quality extra-virgin olive oil over each slice.

Preheat the oven to 400°F. Line a baking sheet with parchment paper.

Carefully transfer the pastry to the prepared baking sheet. Refrigerate until ready to use.

In a large bowl, combine the tomatoes with 2 tablespoons of olive oil, thyme, rosemary, salt, and pepper until well coated. Place the tomatoes cut-side up in a single layer on a foil-lined baking sheet. Roast for 1 hour, or until the tomatoes are very soft.

Brush the Blitz Puff Pastry with the remaining olive oil, then dock the center of the pastry with a fork, leaving a 1" border around the edges. Bake the pastry for 15–20 minutes, or until golden brown and puffed.

Spread ½ the Romano cheese on the warm pastry. Layer on the roasted tomatoes, then add the remaining cheese. Return to the oven for 3 minutes to warm through. Serve warm.

Duck Confit Tart

SERVES 8

2 duck leg and thigh quarters, patted dry

1 tablespoon kosher salt

2 teaspoons fresh thyme, chopped

1 teaspoon fresh-ground cracked black pepper

1 recipe Blitz Puff Pastry (see Chapter 1), rolled out to 12" × 15"

3 cups olive oil (not extra virgin) or duck fat

1 shallot, minced

1 cup sliced oyster mushrooms, roughly chopped

1 clove garlic, minced

To confit is to cook something slowly in its own fat. In this case, you're cooking duck legs and thighs, which yield tender, flavorful meat with a buttery texture. If you have duck fat available feel free to use it here, but this olive oil method produces meltingly tender duck meat that makes this an unusually sophisticated tart.

Lay the leg portions on a platter skin-side down. Season both sides of the duck leg quarters with the salt, thyme, and pepper. Cover and refrigerate for 12 hours.

Remove the duck from the refrigerator and carefully rinse off the excess salt mixture. Pat dry with paper towels.

In a slow cooker, insert the duck skin-side down, then add the olive oil. Cover and cook on low for 10 hours, or until the meat pulls away from the bone. Allow the duck to cool for 1 hour, then remove the fat and shred the meat, discarding the skin. Set aside.

Preheat the oven to 400°F.

Carefully transfer the Blitz Puff Pastry to a baking sheet lined with parchment paper. Dock the center with a fork, leaving a 1" border around the edges. Bake the pastry for 15–20 minutes, or until golden brown and puffed. Set aside to cool slightly.

In a medium skillet over medium heat, add 1 tablespoon of the olive oil from the slow cooker. Once the fat ripples and shimmers, add the shallot and cook until tender, about 3 minutes.

Add the mushrooms and cook, stirring frequently, until softened and browned, about 5 minutes.

Add the minced garlic and shredded duck meat. Cook until the garlic is fragrant, about 1 minute.

Spread the duck mixture over the top of the Blitz Puff Pastry. Return to the oven for 3–5 minutes to warm through. Serve warm.

Prosciutto, Date, and Chorizo Hand Pies

SERVES 8

4 ounces prosciutto, chopped

½ cup Mexican chorizo, removed from the casing

1 small onion, finely chopped

1 clove garlic, minced

¼ cup pitted dates, chopped

2 recipes All-Butter Pie Crust (see Chapter 1)

1 egg, beaten

These hand pies were inspired by an appetizer dish of chorizo-stuffed dates wrapped in bacon. As a cocktail nibble, they are outstanding, rich yet not overbearing, due to the sweetness of the dates. As an individual pie, encased in a buttery crust, this recipe is simply magic.

In a medium skillet over medium heat, add the prosciutto. Cook until very crisp, about 2 minutes, then remove from the pan to drain. Drain any accumulated fat from the pan.

Return the pan to the heat and add the chorizo. Cook, stirring frequently, until the sausage is darker in color, about 5 minutes. Drain off the excess fat.

Return the skillet to the heat and add the onion, garlic, and chopped dates. Cook, stirring constantly, until the onions begin to soften, about 3 minutes. Remove the pot from the heat, stir in the prosciutto, and allow the mixture to cool slightly.

Cut the pastry into 16 (4") rounds or squares. Place a heaping tablespoon of the filling into the pastry, then brush the edges of the pastry with beaten egg. Place a second piece of dough over the top and pinch or crimp the edges with a fork to seal. Place the pies on a baking sheet and chill for 1 hour.

Preheat the oven to 425°F.

Brush the tops of the pies with beaten egg, then cut a tiny slit into the top of each pie to vent steam. Bake for 10 minutes, then reduce the heat to 350°F and bake for 20–25 minutes more, or until the pastry is golden brown all over. Enjoy warm.

Chapter 7

Spicy, Salty, and Exotic Pies

From fresh sea salt and chocolate to lemons and serrano chilies, nothing sparks the flavor of sweets better than a little salt or a little spice. The human palate is terribly sophisticated, and is able to experience different flavors and sensations simultaneously, which is a good thing because the exotic ingredients found in this chapter bring an air of the unexpected to these not-so-humble pies. In this chapter the recipes range from fruity with a warm spicy kick to beautifully sweet with a salty bite. So lick the chipotle and cheese from your lips and let the savoring begin!

Salted Lime Curd Tart

SERVES 8

1 cup sugar

1 tablespoon orange juice

1 cup lime juice

8 egg yolks

2 tablespoons cornstarch

8 tablespoons unsalted butter

1 (9") Traditional Graham Cracker Crust (see Chapter 1), baked and cooled

½ cup heavy whipping cream, cold

1 tablespoon powdered sugar

½ teaspoon coarse sea salt

A few feathery flakes of salt are the perfect companion to the juicy, tangy lime used in this delicious tart. Think of the margarita where the bite of salt helps the lime-infused cocktail taste that much sweeter. In this pie, the filling is pleasantly tart with a hint of salt sprinkled over the top to make it really shine.

In a medium saucepan, combine the sugar, orange juice, and lime juice and stir until the sugar is melted.

Whisk in the egg yolks and cornstarch. Cook over medium heat, whisking constantly, until bubbling and thick, about 8 minutes.

Reduce the heat to low and stir in the butter until melted. Pour the curd through a strainer into the Traditional Graham Cracker Crust. Place a layer of plastic wrap directly onto the filling and chill for 4 hours, or overnight.

When you are ready to serve, combine the heavy whipping cream and powdered sugar in a medium bowl. With a whisk or hand mixer, beat the cream until it forms medium peaks, about 2 minutes.

Spread the whipped cream evenly over the pie, then sprinkle the sea salt evenly over the whipped cream. Serve immediately.

Chipotle Fudge Pie

SERVES 8

2 ounces unsweetened chocolate, chopped

2 tablespoons butter

2 eggs

2 egg yolks

½ cup sugar

¾ cup corn syrup

½ teaspoon vanilla

1 tablespoon cocoa powder

½ teaspoon dry chipotle powder

½ teaspoon cinnamon

1 (9") Mealy Pie Crust (see Chapter 1), unbaked

There is something almost addictive about a fudgy chocolate pie that leaves a little warm tingle behind on your tongue. The chipotle flavor in this pie is subtle, but when combined with the earthy chocolate cinnamon its smoky flavor steals the show. This pie is not too spicy, but if heat is a concern you can reduce the chipotle to ¼ teaspoon.

Preheat the oven to 375°F.

In a double boiler, melt the chocolate and butter until smooth. Remove from the heat.

In a large bowl, combine the eggs, egg yolks, sugar, and corn syrup. Add in the melted chocolate, vanilla, cocoa powder, chipotle powder, and cinnamon and whisk until well combined.

Pour the mixture into the pastry crust and place on a baking sheet. Bake for 30–35 minutes, or until the filling is just set. Serve slightly warm.

Salted Peanut Pie

SERVES 8

¾ stick unsalted butter, melted

¼ cup creamy peanut butter

¾ cup packed light brown sugar

½ cup light corn syrup

1 teaspoon vanilla

3 eggs

1 cup salted peanuts

1 (9") Mealy Pie Crust (see Chapter 1), unbaked

Salty peanuts are a popular ingredient in candy making, and have been for years. This perfect pie borrows from that tradition to create a filling with just the right amount of salty sweetness, and loads of peanut flavor. If you prefer, or if you have an allergy to peanuts, you can substitute salted cashews or almonds in this pie.

Preheat the oven to 350°F.

In a large bowl, whisk together the butter, peanut butter, brown sugar, corn syrup, vanilla, and eggs until well combined.

Spread the peanuts evenly in the bottom of the pastry crust, then pour the egg mixture over the top. Tap the pie gently on the counter to release any air bubbles.

Place the pie on a baking sheet and bake for 50–60 minutes, or until the filling is puffed all over and set. Cool to room temperature before serving.

Raspberry Chipotle Crumb Tart

SERVES 8

1 Short Crust for Tarts (see Chapter 1), unbaked

3 cups raspberries

¾ cup white sugar

2 tablespoons cornstarch

2 tablespoons butter, melted

1 teaspoon lemon juice

½ teaspoon vanilla

½ chipotle pepper in adobo, finely chopped

¼ teaspoon ground cinnamon

¼ teaspoon salt

1 recipe Butter Crumble (see Chapter 2)

Sweet raspberries pair surprisingly well with spicy chipotle peppers, and this sophisticated pie plays with this flavor profile by making use of a chipotle pepper preserved in adobo. Adobo is a spicy Latin marinade that includes paprika, oregano, and vinegar. Those flavors add a subtle savory edge to this pie that keeps it from being too sweet.

Preheat the oven to 350°F.

Line the Short Crust for Tarts with parchment paper or a double layer of aluminum foil and add pie weights or dry beans. Bake for 12 minutes, then remove the paper and weights and bake for an additional 10–15 minutes, or until the crust is golden brown all over. Remove from the oven and set aside to cool. Leave the oven on.

In a large bowl, combine the raspberries, sugar, cornstarch, butter, lemon juice, vanilla, chipotle, cinnamon, and salt until well combined. Spread into the crust and top with the Butter Crumble.

Place the tart on a baking sheet and bake for 35–45 minutes, or until the filling is bubbling and the crumble is golden brown. Allow to cool completely before serving.

Chorizo Empanadas

SERVES 8

½ cup Mexican chorizo, removed from the casing

1 small onion, finely chopped

½ red bell pepper, finely chopped

1 small jalapeño, minced

1 clove garlic, minced

½ teaspoon cumin

8 ounces cream cheese, room temperature

1 cup shredded sharp Cheddar cheese

2 recipes All-Butter Pie Crust (see Chapter 1)

1 egg, beaten

Oil, for frying

Mexican chorizo, a delicious mix of ground pork and spices, is often served for breakfast mixed with eggs. This recipe gives the humble chorizo a lift up by mixing with creamy cheese and peppers to create this rich and flavorful filling. These empanadas are fried until golden brown, and if you are making these for guests, you can make them up to an hour in advance and hold them in a warm oven.

In a medium skillet over medium heat, add the chorizo. Cook, stirring frequently, until the sausage is darker in color, about 5 minutes. Drain off the excess fat.

Return the skillet to the heat and add the onion, bell pepper, jalapeño, garlic, and cumin. Cook, stirring constantly, until the onions and peppers begin to soften, about 3 minutes. Remove the pan from the heat and allow the mixture to cool slightly.

In a medium bowl, beat the cream cheese until smooth. Stir in the chorizo mixture and Cheddar cheese. Mix until well blended, then cover and chill for 1 hour.

Cut the pastry into 8 (6") rounds or squares. Place about ⅓ cup filling into the pastry slightly off center, brush the edges of the pastry with beaten egg, and fold the dough over the filling. Pinch or crimp with a fork to seal. Place the pies on a baking sheet and chill for 1 hour.

Fill a deep pot at least 3" deep with oil, making sure the oil is at least 3" from the top of the pot. Heat the oil to 375°F.

Working in batches, fry the pies until golden brown on both sides, about 3 minutes for the first side and about 2 minutes for the second side. Drain on a rack over a paper towel–lined sheet pan. Enjoy warm.

Strawberry Jalapeño Pie

SERVES 8

1 quart fresh strawberries, hulled and quartered

¾ cup sugar

1 tablespoon butter

1 medium jalapeño, stemmed, seeded and finely minced

3 tablespoons cornstarch

¼ teaspoon cinnamon

¾ cup cranberry juice

½ teaspoon vanilla

1 (9") Traditional Graham Cracker Crust (see Chapter 1), baked and cooled

1 recipe Stabilized Whipped Cream (see Chapter 2)

Jalapeños, which have a mild fruity flavor, have been showing up in pepper jellies for years, and a spicy, sweet, strawberry jalapeño jelly inspired this pie. To get the best flavor possible, use fresh strawberries when they are in season. Frozen berries become too mushy after baking.

In a medium bowl, combine ½ of the strawberries with the sugar. With a potato masher or a fork, mash the berries until mostly smooth. Stir in the remaining berries and let stand for 10 minutes.

In a large saucepan, melt the butter until it foams. Add the minced jalapeño and cook, stirring constantly, for 1 minute.

In a bowl, combine the berry mixture, cornstarch, cinnamon, and cranberry juice. Add to the jalapeño and cook over medium heat until the mixture thickens and bubbles, about 5 minutes. Once thick, remove from the heat and stir in the vanilla.

Pour the mixture into the Traditional Graham Cracker Crust and chill for 4 hours. Once chilled, prepare the Stabilized Whipped Cream and spread over the top. Chill for 30 minutes before serving.

Mexican Hot Chocolate Pie

SERVES 8

2 ounces unsweetened chocolate, chopped

2 tablespoons butter

2 eggs

2 egg yolks

½ cup sugar

¾ cup corn syrup

1 teaspoon vanilla

½ teaspoon chili powder

½ teaspoon ground cinnamon

1 tablespoon cocoa powder

1 (9") Mealy Pie Crust (see Chapter 1), unbaked

The warmth of cinnamon and spicy chili powder makes Mexican hot chocolate a popular beverage, especially when the weather turns chilly. This pie borrows those flavors for a fudgy custard that will have chocolate lovers swooning! This pie is good at room temperature, but it is best to serve it slightly warm. That way you get the full Mexican hot chocolate experience!

Preheat the oven to 375°F.

In a double boiler, melt the chocolate and butter until smooth. Remove from the heat.

In a large bowl, combine the eggs, egg yolks, sugar, and corn syrup. Add in the melted chocolate, vanilla, chili powder, cinnamon, and cocoa powder and whisk until well combined.

Pour the mixture into the pastry crust and place on a baking sheet. Bake for 30–35 minutes, or until the filling is just set. Serve slightly warm.

Salted Chocolate Meringue Pie

SERVES 8

2 cups half-and-half

⅔ cup sugar

¼ cup Dutch-processed cocoa powder

¼ cup cornstarch

2 egg yolks

¼ teaspoon salt

2 tablespoons butter

2 ounces bittersweet chocolate, chopped

1 teaspoon vanilla

1 (9") Traditional Graham Cracker Crust (see Chapter 1), baked and cooled

1 recipe Foolproof Meringue (see Chapter 2)

½ teaspoon sea salt

Thick, dark chocolate cream filling is wonderful on its own, but when topped with a fluffy, lightly salted cloud of lightly toasted meringue it becomes unbelievably upscale. What makes this pie so successful is the varied flavors of the buttery graham cracker base; smooth chocolate custard; toasty, light meringue; and a subtle bite from the salt. Pie really does not get much better than this!

In a medium saucepan, combine the half-and-half, sugar, cocoa powder, cornstarch, egg yolks, and salt. Whisk until smooth, then cook over medium heat, stirring constantly, until it begins to boil and thicken, about 10 minutes.

Remove from the heat and add the butter, chopped chocolate, and vanilla. Stir until melted. Pour through a strainer into a separate bowl, then pour directly into the Traditional Graham Cracker Crust.

Prepare the Foolproof Meringue and spread onto the filling while it is still hot, making sure the meringue completely covers the filling and the inside edge of the crust. Sprinkle the sea salt evenly over the top.

Bake for 10–12 minutes, or until the meringue is golden brown. Remove from oven and cool to room temperature, uncovered, before slicing.

Habanero Passion Fruit Pie

SERVES 8

1 tablespoon unflavored gelatin

2 tablespoons cool water

½ cup fresh passion fruit purée

½ habanero pepper, seeded and well cleaned, puréed

4 eggs, separated, at room temperature

1 cup sugar, divided

½ teaspoon salt

1 pinch cream of tartar

1 Traditional Graham Cracker Crust (see Chapter 1), baked and cooled

1 recipe Stabilized Whipped Cream (see Chapter 2)

2 tablespoons passion fruit seeds

Passion fruit is sweet and very, very tangy, which makes it the perfect complement to the fiery heat and mild fruity flavor of the habanero pepper. This passionate pie is not for the faint of heart, but if you like things with a fiery kick, then this pie is definitely for you.

In a small bowl, combine the gelatin and water. Allow to stand for 10 minutes, then heat for 8–10 seconds in the microwave, or until just melted. Allow to cool to room temperature.

In a heavy medium saucepan, combine the passion fruit purée, habanero purée, egg yolks, ½ cup sugar, and salt. Stir constantly over low heat until sugar is dissolved and the mixture begins to thicken slightly and simmer, about 5 minutes. Do not boil.

Pour the mixture through a strainer into a large bowl and whisk in the melted gelatin. Allow the mixture to cool to room temperature.

With a hand mixer or stand mixer, beat egg whites and cream of tartar until they become frothy, about 30 seconds.

Gradually add remaining ½ cup of the sugar and continue beating the egg whites until they form medium peaks, about 1 minute. Fold the egg whites into the cooled fruit purée mixture.

Carefully spread the filling into Traditional Graham Cracker Crust. Cover with plastic and refrigerate for 4 hours, or overnight.

After the filling has chilled, prepare the Stabilized Whipped Cream and carefully spread it over the top of the pie and garnish with the passion fruit seeds. Chill for 30 minutes before serving.

Chai Cream Pie

SERVES 8

1 (9") All-Butter Pie Crust (see Chapter 1), unbaked

2 cups half-and-half

8 green cardamom pods, crushed

6 whole cloves

1 cinnamon stick, broken

1 tablespoon fresh ginger, roughly chopped

1 black tea bag

⅔ cup sugar

1 vanilla bean, split and the seeds scraped out

3 tablespoons cornstarch

2 eggs

¼ teaspoon salt

2 tablespoons butter

1 recipe Stabilized Whipped Cream (see Chapter 2)

Chai, a milk-based tea beverage, is originally from India, but has recently become craved the world over. To keep up with the trend, this sophisticated pie turns this warm, lush beverage into a cool, smooth pie! While there are commercially prepared chai tea bases available in most stores, steep whole spices along with the black tea to get the best flavor.

Preheat the oven to 375°F.

Line the pie crust with parchment paper or a double layer of aluminum foil and add pie weights or dry beans. Bake for 15 minutes, then remove the paper and weights and bake for an additional 10–12 minutes, or until the crust is golden brown all over. Remove from the oven and set aside to cool.

In a medium saucepan, combine the half-and-half, cardamom pods, cloves, cinnamon, and ginger. Bring the mixture to a simmer, then remove from the heat, add the tea bag, cover with a lid, and allow to steep for 10 minutes. Once steeped, remove the tea bag and strain the half-and-half. Return to the pot.

To the half-and-half, add the sugar, vanilla bean and seeds, cornstarch, eggs, and salt. Whisk until smooth, then cook over medium heat, stirring constantly, until it begins to boil and thicken, about 10 minutes.

Remove from the heat and add the butter. Stir until the butter is melted. Pour through a strainer into a separate bowl, then pour directly into the prepared crust. Place a layer of cling film directly on the custard and chill for 3 hours.

Once chilled, prepare the Stabilized Whipped Cream and spread it over the top of the pie. Chill for 30 minutes before serving.

Chipotle Peanut Butter Cheese Pie

SERVES 8

¾ cup creamy peanut butter

4 ounces cream cheese, softened

½ teaspoon dried chipotle powder

1¼ cups powdered sugar, divided

1 cup heavy cream

½ teaspoon vanilla

1 (9") Chocolate Cookie Crust (see Chapter 1) or Pretzel Crust (see Chapter 1), baked and cooled

1 recipe Chocolate–Peanut Butter Fudge Sauce (see Chapter 2), for garnish

This unexpected pie has a fluffy peanut butter filling that is spiked with a hint of chipotle powder. When you first take a bite, you taste nothing but luscious peanut butter filling along with the buttery crust. But once you swallow, you'll feel a little tingle of heat in the back of your throat. It is that tingle that will surprise and delight those lucky enough to get a slice of this pie, and keep them coming back for more!

In a large bowl, cream together the peanut butter, cream cheese, dried chipotle, and 1 cup of the powdered sugar. Set aside.

In a separate bowl, whip the heavy cream with the remaining powdered sugar and vanilla until it forms medium peaks, about 1 minute.

Beat ½ of the whipped cream into the peanut butter mixture until almost combined, then add the remaining whipped cream and beat until no streaks of cream remain.

Pour into the Chocolate Cookie Crust or Pretzel Crust and chill overnight. Serve with a drizzle of Chocolate–Peanut Butter Fudge Sauce.

Spiced Nut Pie

SERVES 8

2 tablespoons all-purpose flour

½ cup packed light brown sugar

2 eggs

¾ cup corn syrup

¼ teaspoon salt

2 tablespoons butter, melted

1 teaspoon vanilla

1 teaspoon orange zest

½ teaspoon chili powder

¼ teaspoon cinnamon

¼ teaspoon cardamom

½ cup coarsely chopped pecans

½ cup coarsely chopped almonds

½ cup coarsely chopped salted peanuts

1 (9") Mealy Pie Crust (see Chapter 1), unbaked

In Germany, in the fall and winter, the aroma of spiced nuts is everywhere. The nuts they sell are very aromatic and sweet. This pie is inspired by those flavors, but adds a little zesty heat by way of chili powder. This perfect pie is a wonderful addition to a holiday dinner or any cool-weather occasion.

Preheat the oven to 350°F.

Whisk together the flour and light brown sugar. Add the eggs, corn syrup, salt, butter, vanilla, orange zest, chili powder, cinnamon, and cardamom. Whisk until smooth.

Spread the chopped nuts into the Mealy Pie Crust in an even layer. Pour the filling over the nuts and tap the pie gently on the counter to release any air bubbles.

Place the pie on a baking sheet and bake for 50–60 minutes, or until the filling is puffed all over and set. Cool to room temperature before serving.

Chocolate Coconut Curry Pie

SERVES 8

⅔ cup half-and-half

⅔ cup coconut milk

1 tablespoon all-purpose flour

1 tablespoon Dutch-processed cocoa powder

1 cup sugar

1 ounce unsweetened chocolate, melted and cooled

1 teaspoon Thai red curry paste

6 tablespoons butter, softened

2 eggs

¼ teaspoon salt

1 teaspoon vanilla

1 cup toasted coconut

1 (9") Mealy Pie Crust (see Chapter 1), unbaked

Thai red curry paste is commonly associated with savory dishes, but it pairs shockingly well with sweet dark chocolate. This Chocolate Coconut Curry Pie is quite exotic with the toasted coconut, bitter chocolate, and hints of lemongrass and chili pepper from the curry paste. So take a break from the familiar, because this dish is anything but ordinary.

Preheat the oven to 425°F.

In a medium saucepan, bring the half-and-half and coconut milk to a simmer over medium heat. Remove from the heat and cool slightly.

In a large bowl, whisk together the flour, cocoa powder, sugar, unsweetened chocolate, curry paste, and butter until completely combined.

Add the eggs, salt, and vanilla and mix well. Slowly whisk in the warm milk mixture until smooth. Fold in the toasted coconut.

Pour the mixture into the prepared pastry crust and place on a sheet pan. Bake in the lower third of the oven for 10 minutes, then reduce the heat to 325°F and bake for an additional 30–40 minutes, or until the filling is just set at the edges while the center is just slightly wobbly. Do not overbake, or the custard will become watery. Cool completely before slicing.

Ancho Chili, Pecan, and Chocolate Toffee Pie

SERVES 8

2 ounces unsweetened chocolate, chopped

2 tablespoons butter

2 eggs

2 egg yolks

½ cup packed light brown sugar

¾ cup corn syrup

1 teaspoon vanilla

½ teaspoon ancho chili powder

1 tablespoon cocoa powder

½ cup chopped pecans

½ cup toffee bits, plus more for garnish

1 (9") Mealy Pie Crust (see Chapter 1), unbaked

½ recipe Spiked Whipped Cream (see Chapter 2)

This posh pie is a sweet and spicy Southwest twist on the traditional pecan pie. The ancho chilies used to take this pie from homemade to high class are the dried version of the poblano pepper, and they pack quite a bit of heat. However, the heat is tempered by the nutty pecans and rich toffee bits swimming in a sticky brown sugar custard. Top each slice of this pie with a little whipped cream, and you have a unique dessert sure to please!

Preheat the oven to 375°F.

In a double boiler, melt the chocolate and butter until smooth. Remove from the heat.

In a large bowl, combine the eggs, egg yolks, sugar, and corn syrup. Add in the melted chocolate, vanilla, ancho chili powder, and cocoa powder and whisk until well combined.

Spread the pecans and toffee bits in an even layer into the bottom of the prepared pastry crust, then carefully pour the mixture over the top.

Place the pie on a baking sheet and bake for 30–35 minutes, or until the filling is just set. Serve slightly warm with a spoonful of Spiked Whipped Cream and a few toffee bits sprinkled over the top.

Bitter Chocolate and Salted Marshmallow Pie

SERVES 8

2 ounces bittersweet chocolate, chopped

2 tablespoons butter

2 eggs

2 egg yolks

½ cup sugar

¾ cup corn syrup

1 teaspoon vanilla

2 tablespoons cocoa powder

1 (9") Mealy Pie Crust (see Chapter 1), unbaked

2 cups miniature marshmallows

½ teaspoon sea salt

This pie is a grown-up version of the nostalgic s'mores of childhood. To help enhance the toasty sweetness of the marshmallows, a little sea salt is sprinkled over the top of the pie before it goes under the broiler. The finished product is the perfect blend of salty sweetness that everyone from the young to the young at heart will love!

Preheat the oven to 375°F.

In a double boiler, melt the chocolate and butter until smooth. Remove from the heat.

In a large bowl, combine the eggs, egg yolks, sugar, and corn syrup. Add in the melted chocolate, vanilla, and cocoa powder and whisk until well combined.

Pour the mixture into the pastry crust and place on a baking sheet. Bake for 30–35 minutes, or until the filling is just set. Cool the pie on a wire rack to room temperature, about 2 hours.

Heat the broiler in the oven. Spread the miniature marshmallows over the top of the cooled pie. Sprinkle the sea salt over the top. Broil pie with top about 5" from heat about 30 seconds, watching carefully, until marshmallows are lightly browned. Serve immediately.

Salted Caramel Pumpkin Pie

SERVES 8

½ cup packed light brown sugar

1 teaspoon ground cinnamon

½ teaspoon salt

¼ teaspoon allspice

¼ teaspoon ground cloves

⅛ teaspoon fresh-grated nutmeg

2 eggs

15 ounces pumpkin purée

½ cup Salted Caramel Sauce (see Chapter 2), plus more for garnish

¾ cup evaporated milk

1 (9") Mealy Pie Crust (see Chapter 1), unbaked

This isn't your grandma's traditional pumpkin pie! Instead, this delicious recipe takes the flavors of a holiday staple and takes them over the top by adding a little salted caramel. The rich caramel flavors complement the warm spices, but the sharp bite of salt keeps this pie from being even a little boring.

Preheat the oven to 425°F.

In a large bowl, whisk together the sugar, cinnamon, salt, allspice, cloves, and nutmeg until well combined.

Add the eggs, pumpkin, Salted Caramel Sauce, and evaporated milk and whisk until smooth.

Pour the mixture into the prepared pastry crust and place on a sheet pan. Bake in the lower third of the oven for 15 minutes, then reduce the heat to 350°F and bake for an additional 40–45 minutes, or until the filling is set at the edges and just slightly wobbly in the center.

Cool for 3 hours on a wire rack before slicing. Serve with additional Salted Caramel Sauce as a garnish.

Meyer Lemon and Serrano Chili Meringue Pie

SERVES 8

1 (9") All-Butter Pie Crust
(see Chapter 1), unbaked

4 egg yolks

⅓ cup cornstarch

1½ cups water

1¼ cups sugar

¼ teaspoon salt

1 tablespoon serrano chili,
chopped

3 tablespoons butter

½ cup Meyer lemon juice

1 recipe Foolproof Meringue
(see Chapter 2)

You may not realize it, but citrus and hot chilies complement each other perfectly. Why? Because Meyer lemons have a sweeter, less tart flavor that does not overpower the crisp flavor of the serrano. Fruity, tangy, and spicy, they are combined in everything from cocktails to salsa. Now this sophisticated combination has made its way into a pie that is sweet and spicy in all the right ways!

Preheat the oven to 375°F. Line the pie crust with parchment paper or a double layer of aluminum foil and add pie weights or dry beans. Bake for 12 minutes, then remove the paper and weights and bake for an additional 10 minutes, or until the crust is golden brown all over. Remove from the oven and set aside to cool. Leave the oven on.

In a medium saucepan, whisk together the egg yolks, cornstarch, water, sugar, salt, and chili. Cook over medium heat, whisking constantly, until it comes to a boil.

Boil for 1 minute, then remove from the heat and whisk in the butter and lemon juice. Pour through a strainer into a separate bowl, then pour directly into the prepared crust.

Spread the Foolproof Meringue onto the filling while it is still hot, making sure the meringue completely covers the filling and the inside edge of the crust. Bake for 10–12 minutes, or until the meringue is golden brown. Remove from oven and cool to room temperature, uncovered, before slicing.

Salted Peach Crumble Pie

SERVES 8

¾ cup lightly packed light brown sugar

⅓ cup cornstarch

¼ teaspoon cinnamon

¼ teaspoon salt

½ teaspoon vanilla

10 medium peaches, peeled, pitted, and sliced ¼" thick

⅓ cup all-purpose flour

⅓ cup sugar

¼ teaspoon salt

1 (9") Mealy Pie Crust (see Chapter 1), unbaked

¼ cup unsalted butter, cubed and chilled

½ teaspoon sea salt

Fresh peaches just scream "summer"! A pie is a wonderful way to use those fresh peaches, but the sea salt in this recipe really ups the ante. Not only does the salt help spark the natural sweetness of the fresh peaches, it also brings out the buttery flavor of the crumble topping, for a sophisticated pie that's more than just peachy!

Preheat the oven to 425°F.

In a large bowl, combine the sugar, cornstarch, cinnamon, salt, vanilla, and peaches. Turn gently to coat and allow to stand for 10 minutes.

In a bowl, blend the flour, sugar, and salt. Using your fingers, rub in the butter until the mixture resembles coarse sand. Fill Mealy Pie Crust with the peach mixture and dot the top with butter. Top with the crumble then sprinkle on the sea salt.

Place the pie on a baking sheet and bake for 30 minutes, then reduce the heat to 350°F and bake for an additional 30–40 minutes, or until the pie is bubbling and the juices are thick. Cool for 1 hour before slicing.

Salted Brûléed Apple Tart

SERVES 8

1 recipe Blitz Puff Pastry (see Chapter 1)

1 egg, beaten

3 Granny Smith apples, peeled, cored, and thinly sliced

1 teaspoon lemon juice

½ cup sugar

2 tablespoons cornstarch

½ teaspoon cinnamon

2 tablespoons butter, melted and cooled

½ teaspoon coarse sea salt

2–3 tablespoons sugar

Soft apples, crisp puff pastry, and a crunchy, salted sugar topping make this trendy tart unique and decadently delicious. Here, the flavors of apple and cinnamon are familiar, yet the caramelized sugar and sea salt add something charmingly unexpected. This tart would be an extraordinary finish to a dinner if made into individual servings, or as a sweet nibble at a cocktail party if cut into delicate strips.

Roll the Blitz Puff Pastry out to ¼" thick and trim into a 14" square. Transfer to a baking sheet lined with parchment paper. Brush the edge of the pastry with beaten egg, then fold the pastry up to form a ½" border around the edge of the tart. Dock the center of the pastry with a fork, then cover with plastic and refrigerate for 1 hour.

Preheat the oven to 400°F.

In a large bowl, combine the apples, lemon juice, sugar, cornstarch, and cinnamon. Toss until the fruit is coated, then allow to stand for five minutes.

Arrange the apples over the prepared pastry and brush the tart with the melted butter.

Bake for 20–25 minutes, or until the pastry is well browned and the apples are tender.

Remove the tart from the oven and heat the broiler. Sprinkle the sea salt and sugar evenly over the tart and return to the oven for 3–6 minutes, or until the sugar has caramelized. Cool for 10 minutes before serving.

Index

About the Author

Kelly Jaggers is a recipe developer, food blogger, and founder of the FoodBuzz Blog Awards–nominated EvilShenanigans.com. She specializes in creating indulgent recipes that feature fresh, seasonal ingredients . . . and lots and lots of butter. Kelly has worked as a caterer and personal chef, and she also creates wedding and specialty cakes. Her recipes have been featured in *The Food News Journal* and the Cooking Club of America, and she is a member of the Learning Channel's Cake Crew. Kelly lives in Dallas, Texas.